Keeping Love in the Family

Stepping-stones to Better Family Relationships

THE STEPPING-STONE SERIES

SCRIPTURAL GUIDES
TO A BETTER LIFE

—to Life in the Spirit
  The Battle for Your Mind

★—to Joy in the Home and Family
  Keeping Love in the Family

Keeping Love in the Family

*Stepping-stones to
Better Family Relationships*

by

Leslie Parrott

Beacon Hill Press of Kansas City
Kansas City, Missouri

To

Lora Lee

who has been a leader in
keeping love in our family;
and to
Richard and Carol, Roger and Mary Lou,
and Leslie III and Leslie, who
have been her benefactors
along with me.

Contents

A Walk Through: Marriage tends to breed conflict • Resolution of conflict need not be painful • A love commitment is basic in overcoming conflict in marriage • Coping with tremendous trifles

Scriptural Stepping-stones for a good wife: "A jewel" • A better dinner • "A brawling woman" • "A contentious woman" • Three disquieting things

Scriptural Stepping-stones for a good man: "When a man hath taken a new wife" • "Blessed is the man" • "His delight" • "He shall be like a tree" • "As for me and my house"

A Walk Through: If we could only push buttons and turn everyone into loving, sharing, compassionate people • Love and marriage don't eliminate peoples' problems • Self-centeredness • Deceitfulness • Overconformity • Rebellion • Hostility • Inferiority feelings • Emotional insulation • Is there hope? Yes!

Scriptural Stepping-stones: Adjusting to things beyond our control • Sensitivity to the feelings of others • Absorbing the jolts of life

A Walk Through: The "Who's Right?" game • No impartial judge in marriages • The problem of quarreling • Constructive and destructive quarrels • The hurtful power in passive resistance • Marital blackmail

Book Two:
A Bible Perspective on Keeping Love in the Home

husbands • The great mystery • The Christian
and the unbelieving husband • The grace of a loving husband

makes a good teacher at home? • The rewards of teaching

Foreword

Leslie Parrott is giving us a valuable tool with which to strengthen family ties. "KEEPING LOVE IN THE FAMILY" brings with it "Stepping-stones," and this is a purposeful addition. We will find very practical suggestions for discussion that will happen in family settings, Sunday School classes, and in small groups. The book lends itself to this method.

I was impressed by the specific guidelines Dr. Parrott has given us concerning marriage, and certainly the home and individuals will be assisted toward excellence.

As I read this book it was impossible to escape the fact that Les and Lora Lee have a family of fine sons, and now with their families all are models of what Leslie Parrott has written for all of us to enjoy and benefit from.

I am honored to be the one to write this to introduce . . . "KEEPING LOVE IN THE FAMILY."

EARL G. LEE

Book
One

WHATEVER HAPPENED
TO LOVE?

Chapter 1

The Original Dream

Scriptural Stepping-stones

The principle of mutual submission

"Be ye therefore followers of God, as dear children."

Eph. 5:1

"Let the husband render unto the wife due benevolence: and likewise also the wife unto the husband. . . . Defraud ye not one the other, except it be with consent for a time, that ye may give yourselves to fasting and prayer; and come together again, that Satan tempt you not for your incontinency."

1 Cor. 7:3, 5

* * *

"Husbands, love your wives"

"Husbands, love your wives, even as Christ also loved the church, and gave himself for it; that he might sanctify and cleanse it with the washing of water by the word, that he might present it to himself a glorious church, not having spot, or wrinkle, or any such thing; but that it should be holy and without blemish."

Eph. 5:25-27

"Likewise, ye husbands, dwell with them according to knowledge, giving honour unto the wife, as unto the

17

weaker vessel, and as being heirs together of the grace of life; that your prayers be not hindered."

1 Pet. 3:7

*   *   *

"Wives, submit yourselves"

"Wives, submit yourselves unto your own husbands, as unto the Lord."

Eph. 5:22

*   *   *

"Children, obey your parents"

"Children, obey your parents in the Lord: for this is right. Honour thy father and mother; which is the first commandment with promise."

Eph. 6:1-2

*   *   *

"Fathers, provoke not your children"

"And, ye fathers, provoke not your children to wrath: but bring them up in the nurture and admonition of the Lord."

Eph. 6:4

Our forefathers had a dream. They dreamed that every American male would own 160 acres of land that he would clear for his fields, fence for control of his cattle, and then build a barn for his harvests and a home for his family. And here under the biblical ideal, he would live under his own vine and fig tree, autonomous and free. The values of this agrarian society made an impact on the American home that was never abated until this present generation. The American home was Christianized, or at least the values of a Christian life-style were perpetuated at its hearthsides.

The home in those days was central to every important function and event in the family. Any birthday or holiday celebration was always kept at home and focused on the dining room table, where Mother's menus and her recipes were, for her family, the best in all the world. Even after the children grew up and left home and had families of their own, they brought the grandchildren back for ceremonial occasions, telling them en route about all of the wonderful pumpkin pie, noodles, cornbread dressing, or whatever it was that characterized the superb cooking of Mother. Sunday dinner was the biggest occasion of the week. No one ever thought of going out to a hotel dining room for a family celebration because anything worthwhile was enjoyed at home.

In those days no one had ever heard of a counseling center. Most families had an uncle or a grandparent who had special gifts in talking to family members about their problems. A teenager under stress would be automatically referred to this special member of the family who helped work out their problems and, likely as not, had them on their knees praying before their discussions were ended.

There were divorces, but not many because of family economic dependence. All the members of the family needed each other, and they accepted that fact. A man needed a good wife, and each lady needed a strong husband. Parents needed large families to help do the work. Teenagers needed parents because there were few opportunities for running away from home unless a kid planned to join the circus or follow some other career route that was usually thought of by most people as bizarre. A divorced person was unusual in the community and got special attention, even with loving concern, from all those who knew the individual. And the question of re-marriage after divorce was a moral issue that took considerable understanding.

For nearly 200 years in America the family and the school had a close tie. When the land was surveyed in the move west, each 10 square miles had a section of land dedicated to the school district. The school board was elected from among the parents whose children were enrolled in the school. One-room schoolhouses in America became landmarks invested with great emotional content as each family focused on the schoolhouse for the education of its children. The schoolmaster or the schoolmarm often boarded around in the homes of the children. This gave them opportunity to see where the children fit in the family constellation, where they slept and studied, how they related to Mom and Dad, and how Mother and Father related to each other. The one-room schoolhouse may be faulted for its lack of education enrichment courses, but it had another value in the close relationship and understanding there was between the home and the school. If a boy got a spanking in school, he could count on getting another one when he got home.

And there was just as much close tie between the family and the church. Sometimes the schoolhouse served as both a center of learning on weekdays and a church on Sundays. But there was one thing the church never did for the family: It never assumed the responsibility of Christian education. Each family saw to it that their children learned the narrative content of the Bible and memorized important passages of Scripture.

I am not that old, but I can remember when my mother took me into Oklahoma City from Bethany for the biggest day of my life when we were to choose the Bible story book she would use in teaching me the Bible. I could not have been any more than four or five years old. I remember getting down on my hands and knees to examine the books they laid out for me on the floor of the bookstore. I finally chose the Bible story book that had the best pictures and the largest print. It was called *Egermeier's Bible Story Book.* Most days for more than a year, my mother would call me in at midmorning to sit on the footstool by her rocker while she read me a Bible story. She started on page 1 with the story of creation and went through the entire Bible to the Book of Revelation. After she had read a story to me she would then ask for me to tell it back to her. If I were not able to do so, she would either read the story to me again or tell it to me in her own words. And sometimes we got up and acted out the story ourselves until I had it clear in my mind. She did an excellent job of teaching me visualization without realizing it.

My understanding of the narrative content in the Bible did not come from a survey course in a Christian college but from my mother, who felt it was her responsibility to reinforce the preaching I heard in church and the teaching I received in Sunday School by giving me the undergirding strength of knowing the stories in the Scriptures.

* * *

But something happened that changed all of this. First of all there was the wheel. The Egyptians invented the wheel, but the Americans rode off on it. And when we Americans learned that four wheels could be connected with a combustion engine and the horseless carriage was born, life was never to be the same again. We began to replace our barns with garages and then change the architecture of our homes to provide a place for our car on the inside. We began building roads across our nation and with great ribbons of concrete separated our cities into sections, many times with elevated highways. Very early on, the manufacturers of automobiles learned that the annual model change was the best way in the world to meet the insatiable appetites of the Americans, who had developed a love affair with the automobile, especially the most recent model.

And from the automobile spun off many of the major commercial enterprises of the country. The largest consumer of steel products is still the automobile industry. The rubber industry, the oil cartel, upholstery, and high technology all became a part of the mosaic of the automobile business that was superimposed upon the American way of life.

With the car available, the home became less important as a place where the action was. Hotels and restaurants and fast-food places became central to the American way of life. Young people who formerly had done their courting with adults near at hand were suddenly cut loose from all supervision by a set of wheels that could send them into oblivion in a matter of minutes where no one but their own conscience and their own sense of responsibility were left to guide them.

Then something else important happened. A man in Connecticut received a contract from the government to produce a great number of guns. When his friends heard about his contract they gathered to rejoice with him because they knew he would likely become rich and would probably receive other contracts from the government over a period of many years. But when they learned how soon he had promised to produce the guns, they threw up their hands in horror. They knew that he had made a grievous error. They were sure he could never produce the guns on the day he had promised them. This would make the government angry, and he would never receive another contract.

But he had an idea.

He asked each man in the community with a machine shop to produce one piece of the gun in quantity. He gave them an engineer's drawing and supervised the beginning of their work. On a certain day each of them had promised to bring in a quantity of the one single piece they had manufactured at their own place. As the wagons and surreys began to pull into his yard, he was ready with a series of tables for receiving their load. And when each of the tables was covered with the pieces of the gun he had subcontracted, he asked these men who were familiar with mechanics to follow him and do as he did. Going to the first table, he picked up the stock of the gun. Proceeding to the second table, he added the next piece, and then to the third and fourth tables, until finally he walked off the end of the assembly line with a gun all complete, ready to be sighted in and shipped to Washington. And the assembly line in the United States was born.

What the automobile had begun, the assembly line completed. People began to move away from the farms and into the cities to work in the factories. They lived as close to the factories as they could; and when there was no more space, they began to stack their houses on top of each other, and the high-rise was born. People moved away from the farms in such great numbers that today only 3 percent of the population in the United States provides the food for 100 percent of the people plus many millions overseas.

And the home, which was the center of everything important, has become little more than a grand central station where we pass through en route to some place really important. The home for many of us is where we go when there is nothing more exciting to do. But if something is really worthwhile, we get in our cars to go to a specialized place to do it. We drive one direction for our recreation. Sandlot baseball is seldom needed anymore. We are organized with Little Leagues that provide us with real adultlike competition on an organized basis. We seldom cook a big dinner at home because there are too many fine restaurants and hotels that deserve to be explored and experienced. Ordinary eating is done in fast-food restaurants. We go to another place for our cultural experiences and still another for church and another for education. In fact, when we are home, most families are uncomfortable unless there is the piped-in action on several different television sets or videocassette players. The home is where we regroup. But all of the action that really matters is out there somewhere away from the home, where the automobile can take us quickly and in style.

The fact is that in many secular homes about the only thing they have to hold themselves together is an uncertain amount of emotional cement. And to say the least, emotions rise and fall and sometimes fade away altogether. If we keep love alive in our families, it will be because we have made a decision and then provide the follow-through it takes to build our family relations into a bulwark of love and security.

* * *

The foundation stone for keeping love in the family is *the biblical principle of mutual submission.* If someone in the marriage or family is driven to dominate everyone else and always needs to win, the network of relationships is already suffering, and the marriage is sick. Paul wrote, "Submitting yourselves one to another in the fear of God. . . . Fulfil ye my joy, that ye be likeminded, having the same love, being of one accord, of one mind" (Eph. 5:21; Phil. 2:2).

Mutual sensitivity, thoughtfulness, and adjustability are the hallmarks of mutual submission. In the family where love is alive there are no second-class citizens, no one who is a failure, and no one who is the odd person out. Comfortable mutuality makes the home a bulwark of love and security. When there is mutuality in the family, people come home tired and go out again rested. They come home carrying the frustrations of the job or the classroom or "these four walls where I've been cooped up all day," and there are listening hearts who care and can share the load.

* * *

It's hard to get along in the family without *the presence of a good man.* If you want the cooperation of your wife, then love her. When she feels loved the food will be tastier. And when she feels rejected the toast burns more easily. Paul exhorted, "Husbands, love your wives, even as Christ also loved the church." That's a lot of love. If you are going to love her as

Christ loved the Church, you are unconditional in your commitment to give her your all. And by the principle of mutual submission she will love you like you have never been loved.

Somewhere in one of his books Charlie Shedd writes, "The best thing I can do for my children is to love their mother very well." And it's also the best thing you can do for yourself. God does not call on husbands to be rich or wise or famous, only good. Just be there. No one can take the man's place in the family as someone whose strength can be counted on and whose physical presence makes everything better. It takes the presence of a good man in the home to fulfill the possibilities of love and security. A paycheck is not enough.

*　　*　　*

Then there is *the basic need for a woman with a gentle, quiet spirit.* When Paul called on women to submit to their husbands he was not asking them to give up their self-esteem and ride in the back of the family bus. His admonition to women was a family building block resting squarely on the foundation stone of mutual submission.

Nearly anything a wife and mother does can be performed by someone else if the family has enough money. A chauffeur can serve as taxi driver for the children if you can pay the bill. Someone else can cook and even shop for groceries if you can afford the luxury. Others can clean, mend, and even serve as social director and tutor for the children. But no one can take the place of a quiet, sweet-spirited, soft-spoken woman in the family. Top sergeants with voices that sound like machine guns and tongues that can cut like can openers alienate husbands and children, fostering rebellion instead of love. Good-looking, fashionable women may get the responsive glances of both men and women in public. But an adjustable, sweet-spirited woman will get the love and respect of her husband and the cooperation and appreciation of her children.

*   *   *

Finally, the home that is a bulwark of love and security needs *children who have been taught obedience and respect.* Paul said, "Children, obey your parents . . . for this is right." Obedience is not right because the Bible says so. The Bible says so because it is right. And there is all the difference in the world in those two statements. The need for obedience and respect in the attitudes and behavior of children is built into the nature of family relationships. It is better to leave the children out of your will than to leave them out of your love, which teaches them through firm discipline to be respectful and obedient.

There are only two kinds of young people: those who have been taught to be *responsible,* and those you have allowed to become *irresponsible.* The responsible young adult has learned to pick up after himself, clean his own room, and make decisions that are positive responses and not negative reactions. The irresponsible teenager has little or no respect for people or property, and his whole life-style is a put-down on the established family values and ways of doing things.

It is absolutely amazing to me how a half dozen irresponsible freshmen from various parts of the country can find each other on a Christian college campus in a matter of two or three days and support each other in making a game of how to beat the system. The highest goal of parents should be to transmit to their children the best values and the most important priorities in their family heritage.

Whatever influence a father or mother has on a child after his 16th birthday has been earned. This may be why Paul instructed, "Fathers, provoke not your children to wrath." Up through the middle teens a child can be forced to conform. But after a child is big enough physically and strong enough emotionally he will make up his own mind on accepting or rejecting parental standards. And if the father or mother has developed a harsh pattern of unequal justice in the home, the child will go into a state of rebellion as a natural social reflex.

Raising children and living together in a family are not easy. Therefore, it is a tragic shame not to work at the job of keeping love in the family. Every other option is even more difficult.

Chapter 2

What Love Is All About

Scriptural Stepping-stones

"The tongues of men and of angels"

"Though I speak with the tongues of men and of angels, and have not charity, I am become as sounding brass, or a tinkling cymbal. And though I have the gift of prophecy, and understand all mysteries, and all knowledge; and though I have all faith, so that I could remove mountains, and have not charity, I am nothing. And though I bestow all my goods to feed the poor, and though I give my body to be burned, and have not charity, it profiteth me nothing."

1 Cor. 13:1-3

* * *

"Suffereth long, and is kind"

"Charity suffereth long, and is kind; charity envieth not; charity vaunteth not itself, is not puffed up."

1 Cor. 13:4

* * *

"Doth not behave . . . unseemly"

"Doth not behave itself unseemly, seeketh not her own, is not easily provoked, thinketh no evil; rejoiceth not in iniquity, but rejoiceth in the truth; beareth all things, believeth all things, hopeth all things, endureth all things."

1 Cor. 13:5-7

*   *   *

"When I was a child"

"When I was a child, I spake as a child, I understood as a child, I thought as a child: but when I became a man, I put away childish things."

1 Cor. 13:11

*   *   *

"The greatest . . . is [love]"

"And now abideth faith, hope, charity, these three; but the greatest of these is charity."

1 Cor. 13:13

The most important misunderstood word in the English language is the word *love*. A boy loves his dog; a man loves his wife; a soldier loves a parade; and a Frenchman loves Paris in the springtime. On Saturday night a cabaret singer croons about love to a half-drunken audience, while a rock singer on the big stage in some arena tries to be "honest" about love while screaming into a handheld mike and gyrating to the rhythm of the steel drums. Then on Sunday morning the congregation, dressed in their conservative best, stand to lift their voices in "Love divine, all loves excelling . . ." And in all these many expressions of love we use the same word. No wonder people are confused on how to keep love in the family.

In the ancient world they had at least three words for love, all related but each with its own focus of meaning.

There was a word—*eros*—for *physical love* between a man and a woman. That's where our word *erotic* comes from. And this is the kind of love the world knows about most. This is the kind of love that spawns erotic novels with clinical descriptions of the behavior between men and women. This idea of love and its universal appeal to both men and women is what serves as the backdrop for almost all the advertising in the mass media. Writers and television soap opera people who concentrate on this kind of love delve deeply into the superficial, because physical love is just one facet of a large diamond that takes in the full gamut of the love experience.

There was also a word—*philia*—in the ancient world for *the love we have for friends.* It's from this word that we get the name of one of our great cities in America, Philadelphia.

I read an article in the *New York Times* some years ago that said the government of Turkey was going to drop its long-standing restriction and allow outsiders to visit the sites of the seven cities of Revelation—Ephesus, Smyrna, Pergamos, Thyatira, Sardis, Philadelphia, and Laodicea. I saved the article and soon made a decision I would save my money and make a pilgrimage to the places John wrote about in the second and third chapters of Revelation. It was slow business saving my money, so I decided to raise the funds instead. And in a few months I took off for Istanbul and from there to Izmir, which still retains the sounds of the ancient city of Smyrna, which it is. With a driver and interpreter, we began the inspiring journey to such places as Ephesus, Pergamos, and Laodicea.

The last place we visited and the most remote was the site of ancient Philadelphia, which is still a thriving little town near the Aegean Sea. In general the people of Turkey were not that friendly to us, but when we arrived at Philadelphia, the reception was different. There was a happiness about that place no one could escape. All of the spokes on the wagons were painted bright colors. All who gathered around our vehicle had faces wreathed in smiles. They were accommodating in such things as running to get the local priest to open the Greek Orthodox church for us to see. Finally I asked the man who knew the most English and spoke for the others why his town was friendly when most of the others were not. He turned up the palms of his hands in an open gesture and said through his beaming smile, "It's Phil-a-del-phia! We're the place of brotherly love." There is a love we have for our fellow human beings that is certainly different from erotic love but important in the ongoing of relationships.

But there's another word for love—*storgē*—that was important in the ancient world and still is today. This is the word for *family love.* You have long since learned that brothers and sisters or husbands and wives may fight with each other. But if you step in to take on one of them who is obviously the bully, you've got the whole family to whip. They will castigate each other, but they'll unite and turn on you if you interfere. Blood runs thick, and family love can withstand a lot of abuse and still be operative.

So these are the three kinds of love they talked about on the streets in the Mediterranean world of the first century: (1) erotic love, (2) friendship love, and (3) family love. And these were three different words used to express these three kinds of love.

Then came Jesus and His disciples and Paul and the Early Christian Church talking about another kind of love they called *agapē*. Physical love, family love, and the love in a friendship were all reciprocal. Unless the feelings of love were communicated to someone else and were returned with similar expressions of love, the relationship soon died. Even family love had its limits. But in *agapē* love there were no limitations, not even any rules. *Agapē* love was *the kind of love God has*. *Agapē* love is the unconditional flow of God's unbeatable goodwill. It is the love of God revealed in Jesus Christ. Denney, the great Scottish theologian, held up a Catholic crucifix to a Presbyterian audience in Edinburgh and told them, "God loves you *just like that!*" God not only gave us His best, He gave us His all. He gave himself unconditionally, no terms required.

Each of these four kinds of love is interrelated in life. In marriage and family there is erotic love, the strong cords of friendship—some have defined marriage as a high-class friendship—and the enduring love that comes from relationship by birth. And all of these loves are invested with the unconditional goodwill that comes from an unqualified commitment like God had to the world. There is a special quality to love in the family that must be understood to be kept alive.

First, love is priceless. It is *above every other earthly value.* In the heaven-inspired love poem Paul included in his Corinthian correspondence, he compared love to the musical gifts of men and angels, to the gift of prophecy, and the wisdom that understands all knowledge, the vow of poverty, and even to martyrdom. But love won out in every comparison. Love is even greater than faith or hope.

How then, for the sake of all that is worthwhile in the relationships of the home, can we ever afford to let anything happen to love? Love doesn't cost anything; in fact, it can't be bought. Love is not a thing; it's a decision. Love is a commitment. And love in the home will never die unless the marriage partners and family members decide to let it wither from inattention.

Second, love is a feeling. Infatuation and love are often confused. But they are very different. Infatuation usually hits suddenly and leads into a whirlwind of emotions sometimes called an affair. Infatuation may even be a reaction or the response of an emotionally starved person to a lover who requires no continuing commitment.

Infatuation is usually based on physical characteristics or social status and thrives best in a romantic setting where the main focus of concern is on the emotions. Love has its moments of ecstasy, but abiding love is a lot more than feelings.

Paul did not describe the emotions of love in 1 Corinthians 13, but he did use some very descriptive phrases to describe what a relationship is like when two people have lost their love. A conversation can sound like a "sounding brass, or a tinkling cymbal." And a withered love leaves people with the negative feeling of "I am nothing" and this entire relationship "profiteth me nothing."

A marriage needs more than infatuation to survive. Marriage needs a deep, abiding love commitment by two mature people. Paul recalled, "When I was a child, I spake . . . I understood . . . I thought as a child: but when I became a man, I put away childish things." Could it be the difference in marriage between immaturity and maturity is infatuation versus love? Keeping love in the family keeps the marriage on track and provides the spark that keeps the family going.

Then, love is also an attitude. Love is a consistent way of thinking about someone until the flow of positive thoughts becomes a habit. If you love someone, you can put up with a lot and still be kind. If you love someone, there is no need to get envious because the spirit of competition that fosters envy is not there. Love "rejoiceth not in iniquity," for listening to a hurtful rumor or believing a demeaning report about someone you love doesn't make sense. Love "vaunteth not itself, is not puffed up"; and why should it be? In the attitude of love there is no place for selfish, negative, debilitating thoughts. Love just doesn't think like that.

And finally, love is a way of life. There are some things love won't do. Love "doth not *behave* itself unseemly." Love has high standards that exclude deception, dishonesty, and infidelity. Love "seeketh not her own, is not easily provoked, thinketh no evil." The most trustworthy person in the world is the person who has the maturity to make a decision to love someone with the kind of commitment that shows in the attitudes, shines through the emotions, and proves itself in a lifestyle of honesty and fidelity. Love in that kind of relationship is treated as a sacred trust. The marriage and family that keeps this kind of love alive will grow and develop, making each member of the relationship more important to each other.

Chapter 3

Love and Conflict

Scriptural Stepping-stones

"If any provide not"

> "But if any provide not for his own, and specially for those of his own house, he hath denied the faith, and is worse than an infidel."
>
> 1 Tim. 5:8

* * *

"No favour in his eyes"

> "When a man hath taken a wife, and married her, and it come to pass that she find no favour in his eyes, because he hath found some uncleanness in her: then let him write her a bill of divorcement, and give it in her hand, and send her out of his house. And when she is departed out of his house, she may go and be another man's wife."
>
> Deut. 24:1-2

* * *

"Whosoever shall put away his wife"

> "They say unto him, Why did Moses then command to give a writing of divorcement, and to put her away? He saith unto them, Moses because of the hardness of your hearts suffered you to put away your wives: but from the beginning it was not so. And I say unto you, Whosoever

shall put away his wife, except it be for fornication, and shall marry another, committeth adultery: and whoso marrieth her which is put away doth commit adultery."

Matt. 19:7-9

*   *   *

"Be reconciled"

"And unto the married I command, yet not I, but the Lord, Let not the wife depart from her husband: but and if she depart, let her remain unmarried, or be reconciled to her husband: and let not the husband put away his wife."

1 Cor. 7:10-11

Psychological divorce is the result when husbands and wives grow apart, lose interest in each other's lives, and become emotionally alienated. They may never go through legal separation or civil divorce because of commitment to their children, matters of conscience, or sanctions from family, friends, and church. But there they are, living separate lives under the same roof, having lost all the joy and fulfillment God intended when He organized the world into families in the beginning of time.

God intended our marriages and our families to be the center of our joy in serving Him and in replenishing the earth. But, the breakdown in love often comes because of our inability to handle conflict at home. People who can learn to deal with conflict in ways that reduce its tendency toward alienation are well on their way to keeping love alive in the family.

Living together under the pressures of daily demands and expectations inevitably involves conflict. No two people can ever live together year after year without clashing—unless one of them is willing to be dominated without protest. Even then the conflict exists subliminally although the dominant partner may be unaware of it.

Marriage Tends to Breed Conflict

Marriage is an intimate relationship. People are on their best behavior in public. At home they let down. In privacy the partners are exposed to the least desirable side of each other's lives. Acts, such as lack of personal hygiene, that disgust the other partner revive childhood anxieties, arousing forgotten fears and generating new concerns about punishment or loss of love.

Marriage is constant all day every day, even when husbands and wives are separate from each other. Marriage tensions grow with prolonged exposure to irritating sights and sounds or exasperating habits. A child can tolerate physical irritants for limited periods, but if exposed long enough an allergy will develop. Similarly, adults can stand irritating behavior a few hours or a few days, but constant exposure makes them allergic, if not to the pollen, then to the person. Because families live together, irritating ways can be exaggerated. Knowing someone will always be late brings discomfort before, during, and after the event. Waiting for the other shoe to fall can be disconcerting.

Marriage relationships include a built-in component of rivalry and competition. In fact, the twin factors of competition and cooperation are seldom absent in any relationship. Sibling rivalry is most acute when two children contend for the love of a parent under fear of short supply.

Whatever one child gains is seen as the other child's loss. Husbands and wives have only each other to contend with and only each other to blame on unfulfilled expectations. They do not compete for maternal affection but for other scarce resources, such as money, time, and understanding.

Each of the mileposts in marriage calls for new adjustments and new levels of internal strength. Some problems may be deferred, but strategies that work this year will have to be revised next year. Conflict resolution, in short, is a never-ending process as two unique people merge their lives. The resolution of conflict need not be painful. It can be a challenge. But the probability of differing opinions is always there.

Obstacles to Healing Conflict

Immature people heal slowly. They are like emotional diabetics who find it hard to recover from injury. Withholding truth, allowing emotions to fly out of control, and impulsive anger are just a few of the expressions of immaturity that make things difficult in marriage relationships.

Conflict is always greater when a marriage partner is unable to tolerate disagreement. Negative feelings are inevitably aroused by conflict. Feelings are a kind of information to be communicated and read. Thus conflict can serve positive functions among mature people. Mature people learn how to read each other's emotions. Mature people know that what is said under stress may be a short-term reaction and not a long-term attitude. It takes maturity to keep cool so another person's emotions can be better understood. Immature people react in anger while mature people respond in love.

Conflict often comes from unconscious distortions of fact.
For instance, a wife's wardrobe is a threat to some men who need to dominate. Every dollar spent on her clothes seems to be a surrender of power, and every new dress a lure for the admiring glances of other men. The more unconscious the motivation, the more unreasonable each partner's demands become.

Fatigue is almost fatal in resisting conflict. Some people quarrel only when they are tired. Frayed nerves and shortened tempers make it easy to lose control. Working hard and staying on top of our emotions all day in the marketplace can be exhausting. And exhaustion sets a couple up for a sharp exchange of words at home when the work's all done. Fortunately, for this kind of problem, preventive measures can be taken. And at its worst, a good night's sleep is often a sure cure.

Conditions for Healing

Mature people are less defensive about past experiences, their own ideas, and the suggestions of their partner. A nondefensive person finds it easier to apologize and to accept apologies from his spouse. The mature person is willing to admit mistakes and ask forgiveness, which clears away the underbrush of resentment. Buried resentments create barriers between husbands and wives that diminish their feelings of unity. No matter how ancient a resented incident may be, it needs resolving. Resentment will continue to smolder until it is washed away. The only effective cleaning solution for old resentments is two parts acceptance and three parts forgiveness. And this formula gets best results when the partners both

41

work at the job of talking things out with each other. It is a liberating experience.

Mature people are more secure than immature people, which enables them to be more adaptable in making decisions. They are less threatened and more flexible in compromising or making concessions. Well-developed egos are not touchy and vulnerable.

Studies have found that happily married couples are significantly more emotionally stable and objective than couples in trouble. Happily married couples are significantly more mature than divorced couples in several ways: (1) They are less defensive, which helps them control their emotions more fully. (2) Less defensiveness helps couples get over anger more quickly. (3) Lowered defensiveness enables couples to give in more often in family discussions without feeling the need to be stubborn. Mature couples have less need to dominate each other.

A love commitment is basic in overcoming conflict in marriage. The elements of love—including sex, companionship, caring, and mutual affirmation—facilitate decision-making in the home, while unsolved problems destroy intimacy and reduce sexual attraction. Problems in sexuality are seldom physical, almost always emotional and attitudinal.

Loving companionship provides a base for communication and opportunity for talking and especially for listening. Couples who spend time together because they enjoy each other are able to make decisions faster and better because they are not in competition with each other.

Caring about your marriage partner heightens adaptability. Mature people willingly make concessions to those they love. Caring moves beyond mere flexibility into a desire to promote the partner's welfare through generous allocation of resources. Caring promotes generosity. The one who cares becomes more perceptive of the partner's wishes.

Loving partners can concentrate together on issues. The couples who are able to concentrate their full attention on an issue until it is resolved will have a greatly reduced amount of stress in their relationship. A common pitfall in husband-and-wife discussions is getting off the track by forgetting the original issue. An issue will be settled faster if the newspaper is laid aside, the TV turned off, and other attention-reducing devices throttled. Automobile trips without the children have all the built-in dynamics for profitable husband-and-wife talks.

Coping with the Tremendous Trifles

A tremendous trifle is an irritant that is tremendously significant to the irritated party but a mere trifle to the spouse.

To outsiders these trifles often seem very insignificant. They include all of the careless habits such as leaving the cap off the toothpaste, deserting dirty socks on the bedroom floor, or slurping soup. They always seem trifling to the offender who is usually unaware of his offense. But tremendous trifles cause tremendous damage. When reaction explodes in emotional denunciation of the offending spouse, he reciprocates and the battle is on. The fact that the issue is trifling makes it harder to deal with rationally. Major tragedies draw out the best in people, but petty irritants are handled in petty ways.

The real question is whether or not the leopard can change his spots. The indignant partner naturally wants his

43

spouse to reform. If a word to the wise is not sufficient, a reminder campaign is likely to be undertaken. This, for instance, makes the husband feel like he is a little boy while his wife is trying to be his mother. Or, the wife feels put down, rejected, and unloved.

Why do reform movements seldom succeed? Occasionally leopard's spots do change, but not often, because ingrained habits don't respond well to reprimands. The trifling nature of an issue makes it easy to accuse the spouse of being supercritical. If the offensive habit persists, the crusader becomes a martyr and finally a tyrant. Gentle reminders soon become venomous nagging. Barbed attacks result in brutalizing the victim.

One help in dealing with terrific trifles is to provide more private space for each other. Out of sight can be out of mind. Separate bathrooms and separate dressing rooms reduce the number of tremendous trifles for some couples. Separate bedrooms may be needed for a snoring husband. Strategically located hampers will invite dirty clothes. Separate desks or separate studies will prevent husband and wife from clashing over piles of unanswered correspondence and unpaid bills. In short, the irritation may disappear if the irritant no longer confronts the partner.

Another way to deal with tremendous trifles is to drain off the negative feelings. For some couples, humor helps a negative situation. It can become an outlet for emotion although humor must be handled with care or it will backfire. It can be perceived as hostile. An insecure spouse may not be able to take the mildest ribbing. Married couples must not laugh at each other but together if laughter is to be therapeutic.

44

Finally, tremendous trifles can sometimes be desensitized. For instance, with a fraction of the energy expended on a verbal barrage, all the light switches in the house could be turned off. No light at all or mass illumination are not the only alternatives. There is a middle ground. Perfect housekeeping or complete clutter are not the only alternatives in living together in the home. What may have been revolting at first can come to be accepted as a normal part of life.

*   *   *

There is no way to escape the challenge of conflict in a loving relationship. But there are ways for dealing with it that can destroy its sting and keep it from diluting love between husbands and wives. Keeping love in the family includes the ability to deal with conflict.

Chapter 4

Understanding Difficult People

Scriptural Stepping-stones for a good wife:

"A jewel"

> "As a jewel of gold in a swine's snout, so is a fair woman which is without discretion."
>
> Prov. 11:22

*   *   *

A better dinner

> "Better is a dinner of herbs where love is, than a stalled ox and hatred therewith."
>
> Prov. 15:17

*   *   *

"A brawling woman"

> "It is better to dwell in a corner of the housetop, than with a brawling woman in a wide house. . . . It is better to dwell in the wilderness, than with a contentious and an angry woman."
>
> Prov. 21:9, 19

*   *   *

"A contentious woman"

> "A continual dropping in a very rainy day and a contentious woman are alike. Whosoever hideth her hideth the wind, and the ointment of his right hand, which bewrayeth itself."
>
> Prov. 27:15-16

* * *

Three disquieting things

> "For three things the earth is disquieted, and for four which it cannot bear: for a servant when he reigneth; and a fool when he is filled with meat; for an odious woman when she is married; and an handmaid that is heir to her mistress."
>
> Prov. 30:21-23

Scriptural Stepping-stones for a good man:

"When a man hath taken a new wife"

> "When a man hath taken a new wife, he shall not go out to war, neither shall he be charged with any business: but he shall be free at home one year, and shall cheer up his wife which he hath taken."
>
> Deut. 24:5

* * *

"Blessed is the man"

> "Blessed is the man that walketh not in the counsel of the ungodly, nor standeth in the way of sinners, nor sitteth in the seat of the scornful."
>
> Ps. 1:1

"His delight"

> "But his delight is in the law of the Lord; and in his law doth he meditate day and night."
>
> Ps. 1:2

*   *   *

"He shall be like a tree"

> "And he shall be like a tree planted by the rivers of water, that bringeth forth his fruit in his season; his leaf also shall not wither; and whatsoever he doeth shall prosper."
>
> Ps. 1:3

*   *   *

"As for me and my house"

> "And if it seem evil unto you to serve the Lord, choose you this day whom ye will serve; whether the gods which your fathers served that were on the other side of the flood, or the gods of the Amorites, in whose land ye dwell: but as for me and my house, we will serve the Lord."
>
> Josh. 24:15

It would be wonderful if we could push computer buttons that turned everyone in our household into loving, caring, sharing people we respect and idealize. It would be great if everyone in the place where we work would become supportive of us and therefore make our lives easier. Even at church, people can be difficult, including the pastor at times. But learning how to live with difficult people is an important segment in keeping love in the family, and the beginning of wisdom about keeping love alive is a straightforward understanding of what makes people hard to live with.

In the homes where children are growing up, personal relationships have a sort of fatalistic quality. There is nothing anybody does to deserve his brothers and sisters, even his parents; they are just there. At school, attendance is enforced by law. Teachers and fellow students are assigned, not chosen. Maybe this is why every child looks forward to the day he can be an adult and choose the people with whom he lives, works, and plays.

The dream of personal choice often becomes a nightmare. People are people, and in almost any home on the block there are problems because some people are difficult by nature and habit.

Even Paul recognized that some people are harder to live and work with than others; in fact, he said some people make themselves "impossible": "If it be possible, as much as lieth in you, live peaceably with all men" (Rom. 12:18).

Our lives are often locked in with other people in ways that cannot be easily changed. Marriage is not a simple relationship between two people; it opens up a whole network of relationships beginning with in-laws and going out in concentric circles through brothers and sisters-in-law, aunts, uncles, first and second cousins, and "shirttail" relatives in great number. Even buying a family home is not a simple matter. With the home go the neighbors, school, and neighborhood business people.

People don't go to church passively. Church attendance patterns result in lines of social responsibility. A person may like the pastor but find some of the people hard to deal with; or the relationship with the people may be therapeutic while the pastor is a trial.

A job is not just a job. It involves people who become locked into our lives on a continuing basis. By the very nature of life, not all of these people at home, among the relatives, in the neighborhood, at church, or at work will be easy to live with. Here are seven of the major problems that make some people difficult to be associated with:

*   *   *

Self-centeredness: The selfish person is concerned with his own interests to the extent of being insensitive to the welfare and rights of others. This kind of person, obsessed with himself, is incapable of establishing anything but the most superficial relationships.

Recognized in the Bible are the sounds and feelings of a relationship trying to survive amid selfishness. "For he flattereth himself in his own eyes, until his iniquity be found to be hateful" (Ps. 36:2). "For men shall be lovers of their own selves, covetous, boasters, proud, blasphemers, disobedient to parents, unthankful, unholy" (2 Tim. 3:2). "For if a man think himself to be something, when he is nothing, he deceiveth himself" (Gal. 6:3).

Almost anyone is easier to live with than a self-centered person. If trouble arises on the job or in the home, the self-centered person never thinks of it being his fault, even partially. His own unwillingness to see himself in realistic terms makes help very difficult to accept and the possibility for change quite improbable.

* * *

Deceitfulness: The exploitive approach to interpersonal relationships usually demonstrates itself in the efforts of someone to manipulate a person or a situation to his own advantage. In extreme forms this leads to outright lying and stealing, but more often deceitfulness results in making all transactions in the relationship tend to favor one person.

The writer of Proverbs has some pointed things to say about people who act like a friend for private reasons: "Bread of deceit is sweet to a man; but afterwards his mouth shall be filled with gravel" (20:17). "As a mad man who casteth fire-brands, arrows, and death, so is the man that deceiveth his neighbour" (26:18-19).

A credibility gap among members of a family will create more tension than most homes can absorb. Promoting ideas and programs outwardly for the good of everyone when they are primarily for private purposes will sooner or later be found out. Telling part of the truth while withholding vital information destroys confidence. When faith and confidence have been tarnished by irresponsibility, the original feeling of trust is hard to regain, if ever.

Overconformity: There are persons so eager to get along with others they will do so at the expense of personal integrity. Overconformity is often accompanied by a tendency to be overawed by the authority, glamour, or status of important people. The sad result of overconformity is the tendency to be authoritarian and hostile toward those who are considered inferior or less important than oneself.

The writer of Proverbs would have chosen poverty and integrity over wealth and loss of self-respect: "Better is the poor that walketh in his integrity, than he that is perverse in his lips, and is a fool" (19:1).

Teenage girls with limited physical attraction and a strong drive for acceptance are tempted to give up their integrity and moral purity for the social attention of older boys. And Pontius Pilate is not the last man who sacrificed his integrity because of social pressure. Yes-men have swapped their self-respect for a promotion. A person who has lost the capacity or is unwilling to be his genuine, authentic self becomes a lost soul, at least in this world, if not in the world to come.

*   *   *

Rebellion: A tendency to rebel against all authority and to become hostile and uncooperative at the slightest suggestion of being directed by an authority figure makes a person very difficult to live with. Sometimes this rebellion takes the form of flouting all of society's mores and manners in an ill-conceived attempt to assert one's independence. This kind of rebellion may take the form of the bizarre in both dress and behavior.

Both the Old and New Testaments are filled with observations on rebellion: "They profess that they know God; but in works they deny him, being abominable, and disobedient, and unto every good work reprobate" (Titus 1:16). "And Nabal answered David's servants, and said, Who is David? and who is the son of Jesse? there be many servants now a days that break away every man from his master" (1 Sam. 25:10). "Why should ye be stricken any more? ye will revolt more and more: the whole head is sick, and the whole heart faint" (Isa. 1:5).

It is the nature of teenagers to rebel, within limits, against authority. It is an important part of the process of cutting the parental apron strings. But an adult who continues to rebel is a very unhappy, disconsolate person. A man 40 years old who behaves toward his wife as he did toward his mother when he was 15 is still fighting the relational battles of adolescence.

Some adults revert to attitudes of rebellion when circumstances unconsciously trigger an unresolved conflict of earlier years. For those who live with people who have episodes of rebellion, there is not much to do during these periods of disruption but ride out the storm. At least for this phase of their emotional cycle the family member is just plain hard to live with. Consolation may be sought in the aphorism, "This also will pass."

*　　*　　*

Hostility: A hostile person has a tendency, usually when associated with authority persons, to be antagonistic and suspicious. When hostility is openly expressed it creates havoc in a relationship, but when hostility is suppressed it has an equally disruptive quality that results in being gossipy or overly competitive.

Although there are numerous scriptures on hostility, the writer of Proverbs has some helpful insights: "An ungodly man diggeth up evil: and in his lips there is as a burning fire" (16:27). "He that is slow to anger is better than the mighty;

and he that ruleth his spirit than he that taketh a city" (v. 32). "Where no wood is, there the fire goeth out: so where there is no talebearer, the strife ceaseth" (26:20).

The apostle Paul, who many times faced open hostility, has this to say, "Let all bitterness, and wrath, and anger, and clamour, and evil speaking, be put away from you, with all malice" (Eph. 4:31). "For I fear, lest, when I come, I shall not find you such as I would, and that I shall be found unto you such as ye would not: lest there be debates, envyings, wraths, strifes, backbitings, whisperings, swellings, tumults" (2 Cor. 12:20).

Anger in a hostile person always lurks just below the surface. Anger can be generalized as a continuing attitude toward life. Almost anything will provoke an outburst in an angry person. The hostile person is wired for a built-in explosion waiting for an excuse to happen. People whose relationships are locked in with hostile people will avoid some angry outbursts by keeping personal encounters shallow and at a minimum. Keeping your distance and focusing on nonthreatening subjects may help reduce unpleasant encounters with hostile people.

Inferiority Feelings: Every human being under certain circumstances has feelings of inadequacy and inferiority. However, the person whose relationships are dominated by inferiority fears has a basic lack of self-confidence and self-esteem. The result is an oversensitivity to "threat" or an exaggerated effort to prove one's own adequacy and worth by such techniques as boasting and showing off. It also tends to make one hypercritical of other people. Such people are especially difficult to deal with and may leave one feeling like the effort is not worth it.

The following verses relate to the problem of feeling inadequate: "And Moses said unto God, Who am I, that I should go unto Pharaoh, and that I should bring forth the children of Israel out of Egypt?" (Exod. 3:11). "And I was afraid, and went and hid thy talent in the earth" (Matt. 25:25). "The impotent man answered him, Sir, I have no man, when the water is troubled, to put me into the pool: but while I am coming, another steppeth down before me" (John 5:7).

Of all the reasons for being hard to live with, feelings of inferiority are most amenable to the power of Christ. "I can do all things through Christ which strengtheneth me," wrote Paul (Phil. 4:13). None of us needs any help to slip, fall, and fail. This can be done on our own. But for strength to cope with life and to achieve goals, every man needs the power of Christ. Forgiveness and cleansing are Christ's means for changing a man's mental image from inferiority to adequacy.

Emotional Insulation: Some persons withdraw from making the necessary emotional investment in a relationship for fear of being hurt. Perhaps because of childhood experiences, or disappointments in love, they have insulated themselves from further emotional involvement. Such an individual finds it very difficult to say, "Thank you," and almost impossible to say, "I am sorry."

Paul knew about the emotional insulation among pagans: "This I say therefore, and testify in the Lord, that ye henceforth walk not as other Gentiles walk, in the vanity of their mind, having the understanding darkened, being alienated from the life of God through the ignorance that is in them, because of the blindness of their heart: who being past feeling have given themselves over unto lasciviousness, to work all uncleanness with greediness" (Eph. 4:17-19).

56

Jeremiah saw faces hardened by emotional resistance: "O Lord, are not thine eyes upon the truth? thou hast stricken them, but they have not grieved; thou hast consumed them, but they have refused to receive correction: they have made their faces harder than a rock; they have refused to return" (Jer. 5:3). Hardness of heart is no new phenomenon: "For the heart of this people is waxed gross, and their ears are dull of hearing, and their eyes have they closed; lest they should see with their eyes, and hear with their ears, and understand with their heart, and should be converted, and I should heal them" (Acts 28:27).

Persons who have been disappointed and hurt in a shattered romance are apt to make personal vows against future emotional involvement and live separate and withdrawn for all their lifetime. Children or teenagers hurt in teacher-pupil relationships can turn against school and learning even though the consequences are a high price to pay.

Among the saddest cases of emotional insulation are people who once were deeply involved with a pastor and congregation they loved but through unfortunate developments have suffered emotional hurt. Many of these make up their minds never to get wrapped up in the church again, firmly insulating themselves from the joy and fulfillment a good church relationship can bring.

Every emotional investment has its risks, whether in a marriage, a friendship, or church membership. This is the nature of life. The wife or husband who can fulfill the partner's life can also drain it, leaving the dry remains of a sterile marriage. The church that can add a marvelous new dimension to life can under some circumstances also stifle it. For most people the results of involvement with others is worth the risk, but for others, the thought of the pain is more than they can take.

*   *   *

To sum up, the most difficult combination of personal qualities—the one most likely to make a person hard to live with—is a combination of self-centeredness and emotional insulation. Deceitfulness, overconformity, rebellion, and hostility may come and go in emotional cycles, but the problems of the self-centered and emotionally insulated persons tend to stay. These problems are a reservoir out of which other problems flow. A special amount of inner strength is needed by the person who lives with someone who is both self-centered and emotionally withdrawn. Keeping love alive becomes a major challenge.

IS THERE HOPE? What about the person who is hard to live with? Is there hope for change? Based on the lifelong patterns of difficult people, the most honest answer is *no!* People who have made themselves difficult in the past will keep on being difficult into the distant future.

However, this negative prognosis must be qualified. With time people sometimes mellow. As the idealisms of youth are tempered with time and reactions to life become more realistic, emotional extremes are less pronounced. Feelings of futility may contribute to a modification of both attitudes and behavior as years pass by. But human nature being what it is, there is little reason to expect radical improvement in the attitudes and behavior of people who are hard to live with. Behavior responses are programmed into the mind with a memory bank that leaves no room for error. Ordinarily these patterns become deeper and more rigid as time goes by.

But there is another fork in the road. I have seen people changed by the miraculous combination of their will and the will of God. I have seen harsh, unloving people become lovable, accepting human beings. This miracle is not wrought on the passive mind that is suddenly charged by a divine zap. The miracle comes by the combination of man's will to change and God's power to make it happen. Here are the best suggestions I know for implementing the process of personality change:

Accept yourself for what you are. Examine the showcase of your own emotions in the light of what other people see when they look at you. Do not defend, rationalize, or excuse yourself. See yourself as you are. The process is both painful and disarming, but learning to know yourself for who you really are sets the wheels of change in motion.

Find some nonjudgmental person who will discuss these problems with you openly and in stark frankness. God has given us the capacity to gain insight into our own problems when these problems can be articulated in an objective way by an "outsider" in whom we have confidence. It is not easy to find a nonjudgmental person with whom you can become vulnerable through self-disclosure. The nonjudgmental person may be a professional therapist who charges you handsomely. Or, the best helper may be untrained and even uneducated. Whether the listener is a professional or not, the most important factor is trust and confidence on your part and the ability to feel with you on their part.

As much as possible, trace back these unproductive atti- tudes and patterns to their childhood sources. Face the ques- tion: How did these patterns of thought and behavior ever get started? These nonadaptive approaches to life are not inher- ited; they are all learned. Who taught you to be like you are? Where did it happen? When did it happen? If I learned to be negative, can't I learn to be positive?

Come to God for forgiveness and cleansing. This is what John—who once had the reputation for being a son of thunder—meant when he said, "If we confess our sins, he is faithful and just to forgive us our sins, and to cleanse us from all unrighteousness" (1 John 1:9). In the same paragraph he said, "If we walk in the light, as he is in the light, we have fellowship one with another, and the blood of Jesus Christ his Son cleanseth us from all sin" (v. 7). You can walk and talk with God like Adam and Eve walked and talked with Him. God is a spirit. He has the spirit of a person but not a body. So, wherever you are, God will listen and in ways you may not expect He will respond as you walk in the light.

Forgiveness results in the acquittal from guilt. "Walking in the light" results in fellowship with one another and is a long-term experience, a lifelong enterprise. Cleansing of un- righteous motives results in a new set of goals and priorities. Self-centeredness, negative habits, judgmental attitudes, prej- udices, and bad behavior patterns have been a lifetime devel- oping; they are well learned. For this reason, the forgiveness of sins and the cleansing of sin do not result in a sudden perfect pattern of behavior. Some people whose theology is as straight as John Wesley's are still hard to live with.

But the power of Jesus Christ, who can cleanse sin and heal the physical body, can also heal the mind, even the memories. He will teach people, who care to learn, how to be easier to live with. James, the brother of our Lord, understood both the need and the process for spiritual healing: "The prayer of faith shall save the sick . . . and if he have committed sins, they shall be forgiven him. Confess your faults one to another, and pray one for another, that ye may be healed" (James 5:15-16).

Chapter 5

Losing Love Through Stress

Scriptural Stepping-stones

Adjusting to things beyond our control

> "Blessed are the poor in spirit: for theirs is the kingdom of heaven. Blessed are they that mourn: for they shall be comforted. Blessed are the meek: for they shall inherit the earth."

Matt. 5:3-5

*   *   *

Sensitivity to the feelings of others

> "Blessed are the merciful: for they shall obtain mercy. Blessed are the pure in heart: for they shall see God. Blessed are the peacemakers: for they shall be called the children of God."

Matt. 5:7-9

*   *   *

Absorbing the jolts of life

> "Blessed are they which are persecuted for righteousness' sake: for theirs is the kingdom of heaven. Blessed are ye, when men shall revile you, and persecute you, and shall say all manner of evil against you falsely, for my sake. Rejoice, and be exceeding glad: for great is your

reward in heaven: for so persecuted they the prophets which were before you."

Matt. 5:10-12

Of all the roadblocks to happy marriage adjustments, none is more insidious and more universal than the "who's right?" argument. The problem itself begins in the childhood families of the two marriage partners. Most partners learn that a dispute or disagreement with their brothers and sisters over a toy calls for an impartial parent to step in, decide who was right, reward one child by giving him the disputed toy, and admonish the loser to a better way of behaving. In the typical American home, a girl may have expected to win the childhood disputes more often than her brothers. With this pattern of settling differences deeply entrenched in the emotional system of both partners, it is hardly surprising that they should perpetuate the "who's right?" habit after marriage even though it is no longer an effective problem-solving behavior.

In marriage there is no impartial parent to step in and render judgment. Therefore, some partners try to be the standard of judgment in a "who's right?" discussion. Either they undertake to act as judge and jury themselves, or they try to find an outsider who is asked to confront the other spouse and then force a change of behavior.

*   *   *

The fact that there is no impartial judge in a marriage is only part of the futility of the "who's right?" argument. It could be that both parties are right. Stuart Chase, in his book *Roads to Agreement,* cites an interesting technique used by Captain James Saunders, USN, in teaching principles of agreement to a class of graduate students. Captain Saunders gave each class member a small piece of white paper and asked them to chew it and then report the taste—sweet, sour, bitter, or salty. A variety of opinions resulted followed by much argument and confusion. Actually, the paper was the same for all, but the sensation of taste varied with the individual genetic differences of the students. Until this chemical reaction is explained, the students continued to argue about whose taste discrimination was right and whose was wrong.

There is an even bigger reason why the "who's right?" argument is futile: knowing who's right and who's wrong does not help a marriage relationship. In a good marriage there are no victors and no vanquished. Suppose a husband were able to prove that his wife was wrong, would he really want to? Would it make him love her more because he had defeated her?

There are times when a husband or wife has information that is objectively right or wrong, such as directions to the home of a friend. More often, things are not so clear-cut. And in the game of "who's right?" when someone is likely to be permanently injured, the risk is not worth the return.

A young woman complained about her prospective mother-in-law who invited her for a weekend and used the occasion to make it clear that she did not really want the girl to marry her son. She did not introduce the young lady to any of her friends and embarrassed her by asking pointed questions about the girl's family and background. As the young woman later recounted these things to the counselor she said, "That just isn't right, is it?" Telling the young woman that the prospective mother-in-law was wrong would have only aggravated the situation. Ultimately, the only solution to the problem lay with the young woman's ability to find a way to relate to her prospective mother-in-law by understanding the anxieties that provoked her to be difficult. A person can be completely right and still not get what he wants. There is a great difference between winning a battle and winning the war.

The ultimate goal for deciding who is right is to use the verdict to force the partner into a change of behavior. Even if it were possible to determine who was right, it is usually impossible to force the other partner to behave differently or to conform. Being right is often the poorest way to develop a love relationship or heal one that is in bad repair. Love is given as a reward for meeting needs, not as a reward for being right.

* * *

Another destructive approach to marriage relationships is quarreling. Some level of quarreling, from vigorous discussion to violent shouting, is common in many marriages. People who seldom quarrel in marriage are usually from homes where quarreling was not acceptable. People pattern their marriage relationships after the models they watched in their childhood home.

There are marriage partners who grew up in a rough-and-tumble home where they learned how to quarrel magnificently and to make up joyously. They seem to get a heightened level of emotional enjoyment from quarreling. However, if a person from a home background of rough-and-tumble relationships marries a placid, quiet person, there is likely to be trauma in both directions.

Expressing emotions within limits rather than suppressing feelings is a good thing providing the partner (1) takes responsibility for his actions, and (2) receives emotional relief rather than emotional satisfaction from ventilation. Emotional satisfaction derived from saying hostile things leads to further hostile expression and ultimately perpetuates serious difficulties between the partners. "Blowing off steam" is just that, letting off steam. The marriage is not blown off the track and the solid character of the relationship is not threatened when a partner momentarily "lets off steam."

Duvall and Hill in their studies have identified two types of quarreling, or misunderstanding, in marriage: *constructive and destructive.* Constructive quarreling is directed toward the issue and leads to a better understanding. In constructive quarreling people (1) spell out exactly what they do not like and how they want things changed, (2) stick to the point and avoid side issues, and (3) stay with their discussion until things are thrashed out and settled.

Destructive quarrels leave fewer assets in the relationship than were present before the breach. In destructive quarreling harsh words are directed at the ego of the marriage partner and are intended to belittle the person and destroy self-confidence. Destructive quarreling is hurtful and punishing and thus leads to alienation and further quarreling.

Basically, most marriage misunderstandings are a product of the attitudes of the individuals and not a product of the situation. People can fight about almost anything if they want to. Or, they can avoid conflict, even in the face of severe provocation, if they have a mutual desire to do so. Most marriage partners self-righteously insist that they do not start quarrels but merely maintain their own integrity by defending themselves.

*   *   *

Another destructive approach to problems in the marriage is the use of disguised feelings and passive resistance. This behavior is known by psychologists as passive-aggressive behavior. It is characterized by noncooperation, negativism, quiet hostility, under-enthusiasm, and other subtle means of resistance. These forms of passive resistance are often generated by unresolved resentments that have been allowed to fester quietly.

There are some people who have been damaged by childhood relationships that leave them unable to express emotional feelings in normal ways. Some of these people develop devices for obtaining the emotional satisfactions or release they need without ever having to admit to themselves that they were the ones who started the hostility. The least harmful of these devices is accusing the partner of "not loving me anymore," in hope that the partner will have to change his behavior in order to prove that he does. These techniques include playing the role of the martyr plus various forms of emotional blackmail and manipulation.

Traditionally, the martyr role has been more often ascribed to the wife, but it may be ascribed to the husband who feels deprived of authority or control in the family. This technique is based on the assumption that the other person will feel sorry for the martyr and hopefully change his way of behaving. If the partner does not change, the martyr gets the emotional satisfaction of feeling abused. This martyr technique, usually learned from a parent, is a common type of marital manipulation.

*   *   *

Another destructive approach to relationships is marital blackmail. Not long after the marriage begins, one partner or the other finds that the mate can be manipulated by using subtle pressure techniques, very much like blackmail and brainwashing. The wife says, "If you want to have a nice party for your sister, dear, you'll have to help clean up the house," and the husband says, "We could buy your mother a decent Mother's Day gift if only you would take back that silly-looking hat." These are fairly common forms of marital blackmail. But the wife who threatens to withhold sex or the husband who threatens to withhold money are practicing more crippling forms of legalized extortion. In its most violent forms, the wife will threaten divorce knowing that she will probably be awarded the children, or the husband reminds his wife that he had to marry her because of a pregnancy.

It is often difficult for new marriage partners to believe they would ever manipulate each other. They may remember how they were manipulated by brothers and sisters and parents, but the possibility that they would ever manipulate their mate or future mate is almost unthinkable, especially at the beginning. The shift to manipulation does not happen all at once. It begins when a mate first recognizes that his spouse is not without fault. Subtle changes in the attitude take place; and the reaction begins. And keeping love in the family grows more difficult.

Book
Two

A BIBLE PERSPECTIVE
ON KEEPING LOVE
IN THE HOME

Chapter *6*

Why God Organized the World into Families

Scriptural Stepping-stones

"Let us make man"

"And God said, Let us make man in our image, after our likeness: and let them have dominion over the fish of the sea, and over the fowl of the air, and over the cattle, and over all the earth, and over every creeping thing that creepeth upon the earth. *So God created man in his own image,* in the image of God created he him; *male and female created he them.* And God blessed them, and *God said unto them, Be fruitful,* and *multiply,* and *replenish* the earth, and *subdue* it: and *have dominion* over the fish of the sea, and over the *fowl of the air, and over every living thing that moveth upon the earth.*"

Gen. 1:26-28, italics used for emphasis

*　　*　　*

"Not good . . . alone"

"And the Lord God said, It is *not good that the man should be alone: I will make him an help meet for him.* And out of the ground the Lord God formed every beast of the field, and every fowl of the air; and brought them unto Adam to see what he would call them: and whatsoever Adam called every living creature, that was the name thereof.

. . . for Adam there was not found an help meet for him. And the Lord God caused a deep sleep to fall upon Adam, and he slept: and he took one of his ribs, and closed up the flesh instead thereof; and the rib, which the Lord God had taken from man, made he a woman, and brought her unto the man."

Gen. 2:18-22

*   *   *

"Naked . . . not ashamed"

"And Adam said, This is now bone of my bones, and flesh of my flesh: she shall be called Woman, because she was taken out of Man. *Therefore shall a man leave his father and his mother, and shall cleave unto his wife:* and they shall be one flesh. And *they were both naked,* the man and his wife, *and were not ashamed."*

Gen. 2:23-25

When God created the human race, He organized it into families. God never made plans for divorce. The laws on divorce in the Old Testament and in the words of Jesus in the Sermon on the Mount came because of the hardness of men's hearts, which made it hard to live together in peace. God never planned on widows and widowers. Death in the family of Adam and Eve came because of sin. God did not promote a singles movement. Even though there are examples of singleness in the Scriptures, such as Paul the apostle and Lydia the dealer in purple, it is apparent that God's beginning intention was man and woman for each other. The problems of home and family all surfaced after the nature of our first par-

74

ents was changed by their own rebellion. Therefore, what was God's intention when He organized the world into families?

Why Did God Make Man?

A slow walk through the camping and picnic areas of a local or national park raises the question, Why did God ever make man in the first place? The world is strewn with his litter. The streams and lakes are polluted with his refuse. The valleys are cut by his ribbons of concrete, and the air he breathes is fouled by his own pollution.

The violence and selfishness of man has made it necessary to build jails, hire policemen, and finance national defense budgets of staggering proportions. Homes are breaking up at about the same rate they are being formed. Young children are shuttled between alienated parents, and older children are in rebellion—isolated, lonely, and angry at life. In view of the sad situation made of his affairs, why, then, did God make man in the first place?

First of all, it is good to remember that *God did, in fact, make man from scratch.* The writer of Genesis makes it clear in successive verses that God did deliberately, out of forethought, create man. "And God said, Let us make man"; "So God created man . . . male and female created he them."

Beginning in the early years of school, children are taught that creation has evolved over a period of more than 20 million years. First, there was matter, then there was life, and finally there was mind, or man. This is called the theory of evolution, but it is still only a theory after more than 100 years, although it is taught as fact in most public schools.

If the idea of God is rejected, then evolution becomes believable on how man came to be. But believing evolution takes much more faith than to accept the fact that "in the beginning God created" whatever was created, including man.

Second, we need to remember that *God made man for fellowship with himself.* The words "Let us make man in our image, after our likeness" suggest God's desire for creatures of like nature for fellowship. As a result of the first five days of creation, there was a world of beauty and goodness from the hands of God. There were mountains and valleys and great alluvial plains, all covered with greenery. God's favorite color must be green since He used so much of it. His accent colors are shades of red, blue, and yellow. It must have been a breathtaking sight when God first looked at the earth and stated, "It is good."

But a green earth, covered with blue sky and populated with fish, fowl, and animals, was not enough. God needed people, in tune with Him and His world, to live in fellowship with each other and with Him. The imagery of Adam and Eve walking with God in the cool of the day is a magnificent expression of God's joy in human fellowship. This should remind us that salvation should not be considered as an eternal insurance policy against hell, but the opportunity to be restored and live in fellowship with our Creator.

Third, we need to remember that *God made man to be happy and fulfilled in presiding over the earth.* God gave man dominion over all the earth; therefore creation is not all in the past tense. The first creation of the world, and man who lives in it, is a closed book. But in another sense God continues to create:

God raises up persons for specific work to be done on earth. When the time came for the migration from Mesopotamia to Canaan, God raised up a man, Abraham. When the children of Israel needed a leader to bring them out of slavery in Egypt, God raised up a man, Moses. In a lesser role, does not God raise up each of us for a purpose? No person is a biological accident. God has a purpose in the creation of every new life. This is why abortion is wrong. To destroy a life is to say it has no purpose.

God continues to create by *taking a person's life which is meaningless and giving him significance.* A new creation even happened to Moses at the burning bush. Hosea was transformed through suffering, Saul of Tarsus through a noonday experience, and Augustine while praying in a garden. Max Lerner in his seminar on the presidency teaches that every useful leader goes through three periods of life: *(a)* the period of testing, *(b)* the period of transformation, and *(c)* the period of great productivity and usefulness. To fail the test of personal crises and never be transformed is to miss God's creative work in one's life.

God continues to create by *shaping events.* Although God made the world a long time ago He is still shaping events. In the shaping of circumstances there is often an unexplainable shift in earthly affairs that can be attributed only to God. People who live in fellowship with the Father are sensitive to the continuing creative events by the hands of God.

Why Did God Make Woman?

These are not easy days for women. In some industrialized nations, more than half of the women are working at jobs outside the home. Competing in a world dominated by men often puts a new dimension of stress into the lives of many women. Emotional, mental, and physical fatigue are interrelated.

In spite of modern gadgets to lighten the load of home-making, the burden is still there, and the quality of help from most husbands and family is below motherly expectations. In spite of all the new look in family responsibilities, the division of labor has not changed that much. Most husbands still do better at washing the car and mowing the grass than they do at peeling potatoes and sewing on buttons.

And in many homes, the burden of spiritual leadership is still on the woman of the house. Without the organizational skills of the mother, most families would never make it to church on time, find a time slot for family devotions, or keep the spiritual priorities of the family in proper alignment.

But in spite of changing times, what was the original relationship of the woman to man?

First, God made woman because of man's loneliness without her. The disease of loneliness afflicted man right from the start. God said, "It is not good that the man should be alone" (2:18). Even though God made man for fellowship with himself, man without woman was lonely. And God saw that man without a companion was not good. The fulfilling fellowship man had with God came when both Adam and Eve walked and talked together with God.

God showed Adam that friendship with the animals was no substitute for a warm relationship with a good woman. He gave Adam the privilege of naming all the animals according to the characteristics that struck him. "But for Adam there was not found an help meet for him." Animals may help fill the void of loneliness. Some have had their house cat, and many a boy and young man has had his dog. But animals are not people. They have the quality of loyalty but not the gift of communication or the spirit of understanding. Animals are capable of a level of friendship but incapable of filling the void of human loneliness.

Second, God made woman because man is incomplete without her. Without a woman man was not fully himself. Therefore God completed the creative design. "And [with] the rib, which the Lord God had taken from man, made he a woman, and brought her unto the man." Just as man is incomplete without God, he is also incomplete without a kind, sweet-spirited woman whom he can love fully and who can share his life. There is a lesson in the way God made woman. God took something away from man—a rib. Without a woman to love, part of man is missing. The only way man can be completed is to have the companionship of a good woman whom he loves and respects.

Why Did God Institute Marriage?

The traditional wedding vows speak of "marriage, instituted of God in the time of man's innocency." God did not perform a wedding, He established a marriage. A wedding is a ceremony that takes about 20 minutes. A marriage is the spiritual and emotional cement that welds two people together for life. A pastor or a justice of the peace can perform a wedding, but it takes God to perfect a marriage.

First, marriage is the full commitment of a man and woman to each other. A marriage needs two mature people committed to each other for life. God said, "Therefore shall a man leave his father and his mother, and shall cleave unto his wife" (2:24).

After examining 6,000 marital histories, and approximately 3,000 divorce histories, one researcher came to the conclusion that nothing is more important to the permanence of a marriage than determination to make it so. Mature people, committed to each other for life, will adjust and accept situations that in other homes would be sufficient reason for a breakup.

Second, marriage provides for full sexual fulfillment. Sexual satisfaction in the marriage is ordained of God. "Be fruitful, and multiply, and replenish the earth . . . and they shall be one flesh."

Both in the Bible and in the culture, there are two attitudes toward sex. Some regard sex wholesomely as a fundamental of life ("be fruitful, and multiply"). Then there are those who look at sex with doubt and distress because of the strange and sometimes complex fruits of good and evil that it can produce. This double approach to sex has run through the ages. Many of the worst human passions and most revolting crimes come out of sex. But the deepest expressions of love and loyalty, plus the most enduring relationships of life, are rooted in it.

Third, marriage is the basis for full mutual love. In the innocence of unselfconsciousness there was mutuality in marriage. "And they were both naked, the man and his wife, and were not ashamed." Not until sin entered their hearts and they became alienated from God, did our first parents become conscious of their bodies as potential instruments of evil.

God, not man, instituted marriage for the purpose of fulfillment of man and woman with each other. Sexual fulfillment in marriage is ordained of God and is to be experienced naturally and in an unselfconscious way.

Chapter 7

Sexual Purity in a Perverted World

Scriptural Stepping-stones

"Adultery"

"Thou shalt not commit adultery."

Exod. 20:14

* * *

"Adultery . . . in his heart"

"Ye have heard that it was said by them of old time, Thou shalt not commit adultery: but I say unto you, That whosoever *looketh* on a woman *to lust* after her *hath committed adultery* with her already *in his heart.*"

Matt. 5:27-28

* * *

"Sanctification . . . fornication"

"For this is *the will of God,* even your sanctification, that ye should abstain from fornication: that every one of you should know how to *possess his vessel in sanctification and honour; not in the lust of concupiscence,* even as the Gentiles which know not God."

1 Thess. 4:3-5

Sigmund Freud studied human nature for a lifetime and came to two conclusions: (1) that the basic drive in human nature is sexual. He came to the conclusion that this sex drive is awakened in early childhood and permeates the human personality and motivates the human organism over the entire life span. Sex may be sublimated, exploited, repressed, distorted, perverted, or fulfilled; but, according to Freud, the sex drive is always there in every human being. (2) Freud also concluded that hostility and violence are always present in every person. He believed there is a great unconscious part of the human personality hidden from view, like the great bulk of the iceberg below the small tip that shows above the water. And this great, unconscious reservoir that is never still—it generates our dreams—is dominated by the twin motivations of violence and sex.

For many mature people, it seems television prime time has been dedicated to promoting sex and violence. Mugging, murder, and mayhem are portrayed as public games with high stakes for the winners who are identified as those who accept the risks and live or die by the consequences, whether they are the Mafia or the FBI. Adultery, fornication, and sexual deviation are glamorized as the good life, by both the Mafia and the law.

From this slick, celluloid world have come several guidelines for the secular culture, including: (1) the principle of consenting adults, (2) situation ethics, (3) teen sex exploitation, and (4) whatever is fun for you is right. If it feels good, do it. Against this backdrop comes the words of Moses, Jesus, and Paul about the sanctity of the home.

The Case for Adultery

There are three words every Bible student needs to understand in order to apply Scripture to life. The Bible teaches *principles, ideals,* and *laws.* (1) For instance, "Whosoever will save his life shall lose it" (Mark 8:35) is a principle, a fundamental idea from which other truth proceeds. (2) An ideal is a standard of perfection toward which all concern is aimed; such as "Let your light so shine before men, that they may see your good works, and glorify your Father which is in heaven" (Matt. 5:16). (3) A law, in the Bible, is a divine commandment that expresses the will of God. Someone has said that God's laws do not have rewards and punishments, only consequences. The seventh commandment, "Thou shalt not commit adultery," is an unequivocal law of God. It has consequences. There is no equivocation with Moses. Adultery is sin.

Is adultery wrong because the Bible says so? Let's put it this way: The Bible says so because it is wrong.

The consequences of adultery have never really changed. The Scripture says, "The wages of sin is death" (Rom. 6:23). The consequences of adultery are visible on every side. (1) There is *death to self-respect.* Pleasure for a moment is often translated into guilt and depression, which hang on and on. (2) There is *death to a beautiful, fulfilled relationship.* The innocence of fidelity is never fully restored once it is shattered. (3) *Eternal death* is a quality of life that is experienced in this world and in the world to come. There are many warnings about what happens to those who commit adultery. "Be not deceived: neither fornicators . . . nor adulterers, nor effeminate, nor abusers of themselves . . . shall inherit the kingdom of God" (1 Cor. 6:9-10). "Marriage is honourable in all, and the bed undefiled: but whoremongers and adulterers God will judge" (Heb. 13:4). "Ye adulterers and adulteresses, know ye not that the friendship of the world is enmity with God? whosoever therefore will be a friend of the world is the enemy of God" (James 4:4).

Also, the causes for adultery have not really changed. Whatever happened to purity as a way of life? Many believe that modern medicine and social relaxation of sexual standards have been the cause of widespread adultery in the culture. William Barclay, in *The Ten Commandments for Today,* suggests that sexual practices in the old days were dominated by three fears: (1) the fear of conception, (2) the fear of infection, and (3) the fear of detection (p. 161).

Obviously, these fears have been greatly reduced and in some cases eliminated. (1) The pill has greatly reduced the fear of conception for some women; although the pill, or the absence of it, has caused disaster among unmarried young women. Abortion is a sure way to avoid detection, but the moral, psychological, and physical results can be long lasting. (2) Infection has been controlled to a great extent by modern medical possibilities. Fear has been all but eliminated. (3) And detection is no longer the threat it once was because of the general condoning public and because of the big cities where people can be absorbed and their past lost.

But the reduction and/or elimination of these three fears —conception, infection, and detection—is not the real reason sexual standards have been adjusted in our culture. The basic problem goes back to the change in widely held beliefs about (1) God, (2) the Bible, and (3) eternal rewards and punishment. If people do not believe in God who made man, then the theories of Charles Darwin have a greater appeal. If people do not believe in God the Heavenly Father, then the Freudian theories on sex and violence may begin to make sense as an answer to what man is like without a soul. If people reject faith in the reality of the next world, then man may be seen as the highest order of the animals and subject to barnyard morality. But regardless of public opinion polls and cultural conditioning, adultery is adultery is adultery, and it is wrong.

* * *

The Adulterous Mind

The first 39 books of the Bible call for a life of purity that excludes adulterous behavior and holds up fidelity as the standard of God's law on which the human relationship between the sexes is built. However, when Jesus appeared He taught a higher standard of purity that must have been shocking to the ears of good Jews who were satisfied to live by the letter of the law. Jesus proclaimed a new standard: "Ye have heard . . . but I say unto you."

Jesus knew that adultery is always committed in the mind before it is committed in the act. An adulterous union is never achieved until the idea is born in the mind and desire becomes a flame in the heart. The will for adultery may be alive in the mind, and inflamed by the emotions, but never fulfilled for lack of opportunity. This means that a man or woman might be highly motivated to an adulterous relationship but not able to achieve it because of unavailable circumstances. Jesus said these kinds of persons have already committed adultery in their hearts (Matt. 5:28).

What Jesus did not mean is important to understand. Jesus did not reject sex as a basic human drive. In the ancient world there were Gnostics who believed all fleshly desires were evil, including the sex drive that came from God when He blessed the first parents and directed them to replenish the earth. This Gnostic idea of perceiving all matter as evil took two divergent paths of response. (1) Since flesh is evil and we are flesh, there is no way to control evil, so live and let live; eat, drink, and be merry; let your fleshly passions dominate your life. And if God's grace in Christ atones for all sins, then why not sin without restraint? God understands and will forgive. (2) The other path of response to matter as evil led to the ascetic life. Men took vows of celibacy, poverty, silence, and self-deprecation. They withdrew from society, or lived within it without being part of it, and spent their energies in rejecting and destroying all human desires for comfort, fellowship, and sexual fulfillment.

Jesus understood human nature, since He was there at the moment of creation (John 1:1-5). He did not deny or reject the mutual attraction of a man for a woman or a friendly appreciation for an attractive person of the opposite sex.

Jesus was sounding the alarm against cultivating an evil mind. A man or woman of such mentality naturally talks with a vile tongue from a dirty mouth because his mind is perverse. He sees double meanings in the most innocent ideas and words. His favorite stories, like his mind, are dirty. Jesus was also warning men against the dangers of fantasizing evil pictures in the mind. The Bible makes the seriousness of adultery crystal clear: "And the man that committeth adultery with another man's wife, even he that committeth adultery with his neighbour's wife, the adulterer and the adulteress shall surely

88

be put to death" (Lev. 20:10). There is strong probability that what a man's mind conceives, he will actually achieve. This is why it is possible to commit adultery in the mind and heart without performing the adulterous act.

By Jesus' standard, is everyone guilty of adultery? This question and its answer are not easy. (1) Since sin is in the will, lust does not come alive until it becomes a willful desire (see James 1:13-15). (2) The popular idea of a sinning religion has caused some Calvinists to proclaim loudly that no man keeps the seventh commandment according to the standards of Jesus. This is just not true. The adulterous mind Jesus was talking about is not represented by the fleeting thought that enters the mind but is in the will, which cultivates the evil thought and generates a strategy for adultery. It is wrong to equate the adulterous mind with God-given attraction of men and women for each other. Women do not need to wear veils. And men and women do not need to be afraid of each other. But they do need to be discreet, avoiding any behavior or conversation that caters to an adulterous mind.

The Reason for Purity

If we walk to please God, our lives will abound more and more in a life-style of holiness. "This is the will of God, even your sanctification, that ye should abstain from fornication." Harnack, the great historical theologian, said that the Christians of the first century stopped Rome dead in its tracks and literally turned the culture upside down with just two weapons: purity and love.

In the midst of an adulterous generation the call of God to man is still for purity and love via the road of sanctification. (1) Christian purity calls for abstaining from fornication. Although the term "adultery" is broader than immorality between married persons, "fornication" is sexual sin between persons before marriage. (2) In a life of purity, each person is in control of the connecting rod between his own thoughts and the subsequent actions. "Every one of you should know how to possess his vessel in sanctification and honour." (3) Love is the only weapon needed against a misbehaving brother, since "the Lord is the avenger of all such, as we also have forewarned you and testified" (1 Thess. 4:6). And finally, (4) "God hath not called us unto uncleanness, but unto holiness" (v. 7). In Christ, no man or woman needs to choose to walk along the precipice where the risks of falling are greatly increased. With common sense and good judgment we can step back a safe distance from the place where falling is most likely.

Chapter *8*

Love, Sex, and Relationship

Scriptural Stepping-stones

"Thou hast ravished my heart"

> "Thou art all fair, my love; there is no spot in thee. . . .
> Thou hast ravished my heart . . . thou hast ravished my
> heart with one of thine eyes, with one chain of thy neck.
> How fair is thy love . . . how much better is thy love than
> wine! and the smell of thine ointments than all spices!"
>
> Song of Sol. 4:7, 9-10

"So I bought her"

> "Then said the Lord unto me, Go yet, love a woman
> beloved of her friend, yet an adulteress, according to the
> love of the Lord toward the children of Israel, who look
> to other gods, and love flagons of wine. So I bought her
> to me for fifteen pieces of silver, and for an homer of
> barley, and an half homer of barley: and I said unto her,
> *Thou shalt abide for me* many days; thou *shalt not play the
> harlot,* and thou *shalt not be for another man: so will I also
> be for thee.*"
>
> Hos. 3:1-3

"I am God, and not man"

> *"I will not execute the fierceness of mine anger,* I will not
> return to destroy Ephraim: *for I am God, and not man;* the
> Holy One in the midst of thee: and I will not enter into
> the city."

Hos. 11:9

*   *   *

"He that loveth . . . more than me"

> "He that loveth father or mother *more than me* is not
> worthy of me: and he that loveth son or daughter more
> than me is not worthy of me. And he that taketh not his
> cross, and followeth after me, is not worthy of me. He
> that findeth his life shall lose it: and *he that loseth his life
> for my sake shall find it."*

Matt. 10:37-39

The love relationship with all its implications for happiness is a recurring theme in the Bible. It all began in the Garden of Eden when the first man said of the first woman, "This is now bone of my bones, and flesh of my flesh" (Gen. 2:23). It must have been some love affair when "Jacob served seven years for Rachel; and they seemed unto him but a few days, for the love he had to her" (29:20). Paul used the mental images of husband and wife when speaking of the church: "This is a great mystery: but I speak concerning Christ and the church" (Eph. 5:32). John, the writer of the Revelation, lifted love and the analogy of it to its highest level when he wrote, "And I John saw the holy city, new Jerusalem, coming down from God out of heaven, prepared as a bride adorned for her husband. . . . And there came unto me one of the seven angels

. . . saying, Come hither, I will shew thee the bride, the Lamb's wife" (Rev. 21:2, 9).

But most couples today are not conditioned to the language of the Old Testament's poetic expressions on love, or the New Testament's analogy of the bride and groom as the counterparts of the Church and the coming Christ. Most married couples are concerned with the full dimensions of happiness that love and marriage may mean to them at their particular age and status in life. In these four scriptural passages there are four centers of concern that can be understood by every married couple: (1) The dimension of sexual attraction, (2) the dimension of self-giving love, (3) the dimension of God's love, which seeks no vengeance and asks no reward, and (4) the dimension of total commitment.

Sexual Attraction

The Song of Solomon is final proof that the Bible is not a prudish book. It accepts human sexuality and is fully aware of the meaning and implications of sex and lust. With the dimension of sexual attraction there are implications that make as much sense now as they did in the ancient world of the Middle East.

First, love and beauty are in the eye of the beholder. "Thou art all fair, my love; there is no spot in thee" (4:7). All love is dependent on God's love. Without God as the Source there is no love. We do not love because there is something in us that makes us loving, but because God is love. God creates love in us. All love is a response to Him. "Herein is love, not that we loved God, but that he loved us" (1 John 4:10). This is why there is beauty and loveliness in anyone who is loved. Love is in the eye of the beholder.

Second, there is a self-giving dimension in love that is exclusive. "Come with me" (4:8). The shepherd lad wanted the maiden all to himself, exclusive of everyone else, that he might bestow on her all of his love. There are three ways in which the physical side of love finds expression in the Song of Solomon, and in life:

There is the natural *biological response to love* that is present in couples because God directed them to replenish the earth. In spite of widespread popular emphasis on singles today, it is just a fact that God made man and woman for each other and then organized the human race into families. Marriage is the natural, God-given plan for man and woman.

Love expresses itself in *romantic relationships.* Love songs, poetry, soft breezes, pleasant aromas, and lovely evenings all feed the fires of a romantic relationship.

Love expresses itself in *redemptive ways.* To belong exclusively to someone is to be prepared for a remarkably renewing experience. A bride is adorned. Her eyes sparkle, her smile inspires, the chemistry of her body and soul draw like a magnet. Her life is tranfused by love. And her love in turn transforms her groom.

Third, with love, there is the dimension of extravagance. "Thou hast ravished my heart with one of thine eyes, with one chain of thy neck" (4:9). Love is extravagant in its *language*—flowery, superlative, even gushy. Love is extravagant with its *time.* Minutes flow into hours and hours flow in and out of each other as lovers become oblivious to time. Love is extravagant with its *giving.*

Finally, there is a dimension of physical attraction and response in love between the sexes. "How much better is thy love than wine! and the smell of thine ointments than all spices!" (v. 10). There is in this Song from Solomon the passionate language of the devotion of a man for a maid. The sensual language in some sections of the song may not have sounded to Oriental ear as it does to ours. But, whatever the reader's reaction to the love passages in the Song of Solomon, the physical attraction of a husband and wife for each other cannot be ignored or played down.

Unconditional Fidelity

The story of Hosea and his love for a wayward wife, whose infidelities resulted in her final sale as a slave, is heartening. When Hosea could have been outraged, invoking the law that gave him the right to have her stoned, he continued to pour out his self-giving love even when it was spurned and rejected. From this paragraph there are lessons for marriages in the 20th century.

First, there is unconditional acceptance in self-giving love. "Go yet, love a woman . . . yet an adulteress, according to the love of the Lord" (Hos. 3:1). The principle of unconditional acceptance applies in every relationship in the family: *(a)* Hosea gave unconditional acceptance to a wayward wife, not because she deserved it, but because she was his wife, for better or worse. *(b)* Parents do not love their children because their behavior is impeccable, but because they are their children. *(c)* Parents are not always perfect either, but we love them because they are ours.

Second, no price is asked in unconditional love. "So I bought her to me for fifteen pieces of silver, and for an homer of barley, and an half homer of barley" (3:2). The price Hosea paid for the return of his wife was probably the going rate for a slave. And it could be he paid a premium of additional barley because of the law of supply and demand. He didn't want just any slave, he wanted the one who was his wife. But what this transaction means is that love asks no price. Whatever it takes is what love gives.

Third, unconditional love always makes itself vulnerable. "Thou shalt abide for me many days . . . and thou shalt not be for another man: so will I also be for thee" (3:3). Hosea made it clear to Gomer that she was to stay home and be loyal to him, but he had no insurance against her future waywardness, for love is always vulnerable. He would keep on loving her whether or not she had the capacity to be loyal to him.

How Far Can Love Go?

Hosea could never have done what he did on the basis of physical, sexual attraction alone. What he did could not have been done from the perspective of human love. What loveliness could he have found in a wretched female slave? In seeking his wife and taking her back, Hosea was demonstrating the divine love of God for wayward Israel. God's love has at least three dimensions that need to be understood by people committed to keeping love alive in the family.

First, in God's love there is no vengeance. "I will not execute the fierceness of mine anger" (11:9). The ways of Israel, like the ways of Gomer, could have justified a hasty vengeance. But God promised, "I will not return to destroy Ephraim: for I am God." The important marks in God's love can be identified in the love of a strong marriage.

Again, in God's love there is an unbeatable and undeserved goodwill. Husbands and wives who try to discipline each other by giving and withdrawing their love will always be in a state of emotional stress. God's love in a marriage is manifest when the man and woman relax into a mutuality that goes on loving in spite of the response of each other at a given moment. Divine love is a fixed disposition of resolute goodwill.

And third, God's love is never withdrawn even when it is misunderstood. Hosea discovered, centuries before Christ, that divine love goes out to us without demands or restrictions, even when we don't deserve it and with no expiration date, just because God is love. When we say that God loves man, we are not told what man is like but what God is like. And that is the ideal love toward which we stretch in the family.

The Miracle of Total Commitment

The three verses that make up this paragraph from Matthew say one thing clearly: The final, fulfilling dimension of love is total commitment. The world does not need more liberal statutes to ease the pain of divorce, but a more liberal commitment to the permanence of the marriage vow.

Total commitment in marriage is stronger than love for father and mother. God has made it clear that a man is to leave his father and mother and to cleave to his wife. This concept is like the welding of two pieces of metal together. Two strong people cleaving to each other will make a strong marriage.

Total commitment overcomes problems that otherwise destroy marriages. Jesus speaks clearly: "He that taketh not his cross, and followeth after me, is not worthy of me" (Matt. 10:38). Total commitment does not exclude the possibility of a cross to bear or a thorn in the flesh, but it does include unconditional faithfulness to each other.

Only in total commitment does a marriage become fulfilled. "He that findeth his life shall lose it: and he that loseth his life for my sake shall find it," declared our Lord (v. 39). There is only one way to have a spiritually fulfilled life, and that is to lose yourself in Christ. And there is only one way to have a fulfilled marriage, and that is to lose yourself in each other. This does not mean that you abdicate your personality. It means that two strong persons find in marriage their fulfillment in helping each other become the persons God can make them to become. Marriage is a high-class friendship plus all the overtones of God-given sexuality.

Chapter 9

The Christian Family Model

Scriptural Stepping-stones

"Submitting . . . one to another"

> "Submitting yourselves one to another in the fear of God. Wives, submit yourselves unto your own husbands, as unto the Lord. For the husband is the head of the wife, even as Christ is the head of the church: and he is the saviour of the body. Therefore *as the church is subject unto Christ, so let the wives be to their own husbands in every thing."*

Eph. 5:21-24

*   *   *

"As Christ also loved"

> *"Husbands, love your wives,* even *as Christ also loved* the church, *and gave* himself for it; *that he might sanctify and cleanse it* with the washing of water by the word, *that he might present it to himself a glorious church,* not having spot, or wrinkle, or any such thing; but *that it should be holy and without blemish.* So ought men to love their wives as their own bodies. He that loveth his wife loveth himself. For no man ever yet hated his own flesh; but nourisheth and cherisheth it, even as the Lord the church: for we are members of his body, of his flesh, and of his bones. For this cause shall a man leave his father

and mother, and shall be joined unto his wife, and they two shall be one flesh."

Eph. 5:25-31

* * *

"This is a great mystery"

"This is a *great mystery:* but I speak concerning Christ and the church. Nevertheless let every one of you in particular *so love his wife even as himself;* and the *wife see that she reverence her husband.*"

Eph. 5:32-33

* * *

"Your chaste conversation"

"Likewise, ye wives, be in subjection to your own husbands; that, if any obey not the word, they also may without the word *be won by the conversation of the wives;* while they *behold your chaste conversation* coupled with fear."

1 Pet. 3:1-2

* * *

"The grace of life"

"Likewise, ye husbands, dwell with them according to knowledge, *giving honour unto the wife,* as unto the weaker vessel, and as being *heirs together of the grace of life;* that your *prayers be not hindered.*"

1 Pet. 3:7

God the Father is the central Figure in the drama of creation. (1) God made man from the dust of His earth. (2) God saw that man was incomplete in himself and made woman from him. (3) God blessed the first pair and put the earth in their care. (4) God directed the first couple to replenish the earth.

It should be no surprise, then, that New Testament writers such as Paul would use the analogy of the bride and groom to explain the relationship of Christ and the Church, and to explain the ideal of a husband-and-wife relationship. For persons looking for a spiritual pattern for marriage, Christ is the Person to watch.

The Principle of Mutual Submission

At the very center of the fulfilling marriage is the practice of mutual submission. Any couple involved in a struggle to see who is going to dominate the marriage relationship is fighting a no-win battle. And any wife or husband who has given up the struggle and has settled for being a second-class citizen in the family relationship has a sick marriage.

This principle of mutual submission, or adjustment, runs through all the New Testament discussions on home and family. "Submitting yourselves one to another in the fear of God" is the alpha and omega of family relationships. Until all members of the household, including the children, the parents, and relatives in the house, learn how to adjust to the needs of each other, there never can be peace and joy at home.

The Wisdom of a Woman

No home can ever be fulfilled unless there is a sweet-spirited female in the house. A rich woman can hire people to do almost everything she has to do. She can hire a cook and a maid. If she is rich enough she can hire a seamstress to darn the socks and a laundress to wash them. She may even be able to hire a chauffeur to drive her children to and from school and to all their other appointments. But no one can take her place as a devoted, loving wife (and mother) who makes the whole family feel better just because she is there.

In many healthy marriages, the wife's role is more submissive than aggressive toward her husband. Angry, dominating females do not make good marriage partners. And neither do strong-willed, egocentric men. The directive "Wives, submit yourselves unto your own husbands, as unto the Lord" and others similar to it have been misused by men who want to dominate their wives without earning their loyalty by their overwhelming love for them. Whatever else Paul meant by this directive, it was not to put women into subjection or servitude to their husbands. No marriage is ever really happy until the husband and wife accept each other on an equal basis of submission.

In most healthy marriages the husband assumes a leadership role in harmony with the gifts and graces of his wife. Paul writes, "The husband is the head of the wife," and there are several reasons why most men are leaders in their families. These include: (1) their sheer physical size and strength, (2) the wider experience of man in the working world, and (3) tradition. However, the strength and expertise of the wife are a vital consideration in the balance of leadership roles in the home. In most happy marriages the leadership shifts from husband to wife and even children according to expertise and who is to be most involved in the consequences of the decision.

A Word for Husbands

No home can ever be all it was intended to be without the presence of a kind and good man. Men who see their wives as second-class citizens, intended primarily to serve the purposes of the man, are neither loving nor kind in their attitudes in the home. Men who think little children are to be miniature adults who only speak when spoken to, are not only ignorant about child growth and development but also hard to live with. In this passage Paul has three words of guidance for men who want to live in mutual submission with their wives.

First, husbands, love your wife as fully as you know how. "Husbands, love your wives, even as Christ also loved the church, and gave himself for it." Any man who loves his wife in the same way Christ loved the Church will never have a worry about her submissiveness.

Second, meet the needs and desires of your wife as fully as you meet your own needs. "So ought men to love their wives as their own bodies." Thoughtful men keep their bodies (1) rested, (2) relaxed, (3) nourished, (4) comfortable, (5) protected, and (6) well groomed. The least they can do is help their wife do the same, and even more.

And third, separate yourself emotionally from your parents or anyone else who tends to come ahead of your wife. "For this cause shall a man leave his father and mother, and shall be joined unto his wife, and they two shall be one flesh." Some men marry but never leave home emotionally. Their thoughts and actions are dominated by the desire of their parents. And some men allow their job or their recreational involvements to become surrogate parents who dominate their lives ahead of their wives.

The Great Mystery

After everything about love and marriage has been studied, analyzed, and explained, the bond between a man and a woman is still a great mystery that defies explanation. It is like the relationship between Christ and the Church. It is an enigma. The depth and meaning of the love of God in Christ Jesus as revealed to the Church is a reality whether or not it is ever understood. And where there is love between marriage partners the mystery of the relationship does not wipe out the reality. The great fulfillment of life is not to be found in fame, fortune, or personal achievement, but in the mystery of a loving partnership and relationship in marriage.

The Christian and the Unbelieving Husband

One of the difficult relationships in life is marriage between a Christian and an unbeliever. The question is, What is a believing wife to do? Peter gives three answers.

Allow your husband to be your husband. The wife must find ways of adjusting to her husband. "Wives, be in subjection to your own husbands . . . if any obey not the word." The wife may have married her husband before she was converted. Or he may have turned from the faith. In either case the response of the Christian wife to her unconverted husband is the same: Make the best adjustment you can. But lack of Christian faith is not grounds for divorce.

Allow your conversation to be its own ministry of grace. The wife who is married to an unconverted husband needs to be especially careful in her manner of life. "They also may . . . be won by the conversation of the wives; while they behold your chaste conversation." Unsaved men with Christian wives will be driven farther from Christ by self-righteous wives who preach at them and nag at their unacceptable ways. An angry woman with a sharp tongue can keep an unconverted man from going to church if he relates her bad disposition to her regular church attendance.

Allow your life-style to demonstrate your respect. Wives with unconverted husbands need to be motivated consciously to be respectful and ladylike. The unsaved husband may also be "won by . . . your chaste conversation coupled with fear." "Fear" in this usage means "respect." It is the quality of attitude that makes a woman a lady, and a man a gentleman. Courtesy and kindness, which come out of a respectful attitude, are like the air in a cushion. Of itself air is nothing, but it sure does help take the jolts out of life. A loving wife who adjusts to her husband, whose conversation is in good taste, coupled with respect and courtesy, is a long way down the road toward leading her unsaved husband to Christ. The style of life Peter outlines for the wife should be dictated by the heart devoted to Christ, not by the whims and fancies of the world of fashion (see 1 Pet. 3:1-7). And the same good sense applies to husbands in reverse.

The Grace of a Loving Husband

The responses of Peter concerning the way a good man relates to his wife are inspiring. Peter's wife is not mentioned in Scripture, although Jesus healed his mother-in-law in Capernaum, where they apparently lived together in the same house. Since Peter the fisherman was a colorful character, the question is intriguing as to what kind of husband and son-in-law he must have been.

105

Understanding: "Husbands, dwell with them according to knowledge." To a man who works away from home on an eight-hour schedule, the confinements of a house and the demands of small children can seem far removed from the real world. It is easy to come home with unrealistic expectations and with an equally blind spot on the sights and sounds of a home where a wife and children have been confined all day. Or it is equally bad to lack understanding for a working woman who comes home to the role of wife and mother after living out her role on the job all day. Every woman needs the understanding of a considerate man.

Appreciation: A husband needs to seek all the ways he can to express appreciation to his wife for all she does for him and the family. "Likewise, ye husbands . . . giving honour unto the wife." Few things fire up the energy and put sparkle in the eyes of a wife more than a little honest appreciation and recognition by her husband that she is a worthwhile and needed person. By nature women are more sensitive and emotional than most men. Their needs for recognition and approval from their husbands are a high concern. A priority item in husband-wife love growth is in tangible expressions of appreciation. There is reason why the flower, candy, and greeting card industries gross billions each year. An evening out may be better than a weekend and a single rose may do more than a paycheck.

Spiritual responsibility: Husbands need to carry their full share of the spiritual load in the home, "being heirs together of the grace of life." Some husbands pride themselves in bringing home their paychecks to their wives, who then have full authority and responsibility for management and spending. Some husbands sit back to wait on their wives to pick up the leadership role in all spiritual and church-related matters. Some husbands leave all of the cultural and aesthetic side of family living to the leadership of their wives. How wonderful it is to see a husband who shares fully with his wife in what Peter calls the "grace of life"!

Prayerfulness: But how can a good husband insure open channels between himself and God? First, he may plan *moments of quietness* and prayer each day at the same time and place. For some people this is done in the morning. For others, it is the last thing at night. One man I knew had his quiet time each noon behind the orange boxes in the warehouse. He also may *begin reading* a version or a paraphrase of the Scriptures a paragraph or a chapter each day. He may *secure a notebook* to use at the end of each day's Scripture reading. One way to start your own journal and stimulate devotional thought is to write this question at the top of the page: What is the Holy Spirit trying to say to me today in this passage? Write down the Bible reference of the passage and then answer the question. Also, he needs to remember *prayer is a two-way street.* Don't talk God to death. Use a significant part of your prayer time listening to what He has to say to you. And *keep yourself honest.* Don't lie to God and don't try to kid yourself. Being honest is the best maintenance tool there is for keeping the channels open that would otherwise hinder many husbands' prayers.

Chapter 10

More than a Mother
and Better than a Father

Scriptural Stepping-stones

"When your children shall ask"

"And those twelve stones, which they took out of Jordan, did Joshua pitch in Gilgal. And he spake unto the children of Israel, saying, *When your children shall ask their fathers in time to come, saying, What mean these stones? Then ye shall let your children know,* saying, Israel came over this Jordan on dry land. For the Lord your God dried up the waters of Jordan from before you, until ye were passed over, as the Lord your God did to the Red sea, which he dried up from before us, until we were gone over: that all the people of the earth might know the hand of the Lord, that it is mighty: that ye might fear the Lord your God for ever."

Josh. 4:20-24

*　　*　　*

"My dearly beloved son"

"Paul, an apostle of Jesus Christ by the will of God, according to the promise of life which is in Christ Jesus, *to Timothy, my dearly beloved son:* Grace, mercy, and peace, from God the Father and Christ Jesus our Lord. I thank God, whom I serve from my forefathers with pure conscience, that without ceasing *I have remembrance of thee in my prayers* night and day; greatly *desiring to see thee, being mindful of thy tears,* that I may be filled with joy; when I *call to remembrance the unfeigned faith that is in thee, which dwelt first in thy grandmother Lois, and thy mother Eunice;* and I am persuaded that in thee also."

2 Tim. 1:1-5

*   *   *

"From a child thou hast known"

> "But continue thou in the things which thou hast learned and hast been assured of, *knowing of whom thou hast learned them;* and that *from a child thou hast known the holy scriptures,* which are able to make thee wise unto salvation through faith which is in Christ Jesus."

2 Tim. 3:14-15

The greatest teachers are not in classrooms. They are in homes. The greatest teachers do not develop course outlines, give examinations, and distribute report cards. The greatest teachers are parents who have become models for their children. They are more than a mother and better than a father. Most healthy couples can become parents, but it takes a lot more to become teachers of your own children.

Parents are the curriculum, and the home is the classroom. By the time a child is old enough to test the views and values of parents against other standards in the culture, he is already impacted for life by the adults whose opinions he cares about—usually Mother and Father—during the first dozen years of his life.

The time Mother and Father have with the child far off-sets any time spent in public school, Sunday School, or church. Children take the problems of home to school instead of projecting school problems on the family. If the family is a warm, loving, secure experience for the child, that security will soon alleviate and even obliterate the problems the child experiences at school. However, if the level of warmth, love, and security at home is low, then the child will turn to the options school offers, including gang membership and com-radeship with other students who also suffer from parental distance and are ripe for rebellion.

The impact of parental models continues to be a factor in adult behavior even after parents are dead and gone. Consciously or unconsciously, a grown man or woman will often behave as though Mother or Father were watching. Adult decision making is often a response or a reaction to the values of parental models long after the models are gone.

This incredible influence of parents on children makes the Scripture an important sourcebook for the pattern and the performance of parents as teachers, including (1) concern for our roots, (2) the importance of our teachers, and (3) the quality of the curriculum.

Begin with Your Roots

Alex Haley's book *Roots* stirred a desire within millions of people in Western countries to know where they came from. This desire for roots is good. "When do we start to train a child?" Someone answered, "Fifty years before he is born." By the time a child can speak the language of the culture into which he is born, he is the victim of it. A child has just about as much chance to change his culture as a baby does to get the unintelligible syllables of his baby talk accepted into regular adult conversation.

Cultural determinism is the phrase used to describe the impact of the people and the situation into which we were born. A boy who grows up under the influence of Hollywood and Vine in southern California will never fully understand the person who grows up in a country church in Brown County, Indiana. And the feeling will be mutual. The contrasts between the two settings into which the two boys were born makes lifelong differences in the way they think and feel about many key words in their lives, such as (1) *father,* (2) *home,* (3) *food,* (4) *grandparents,* (5) *mother,* (6) *school,* (7) *sheriff,* (8) *church,* (9) *music,* (10) *baby,* and many more.

Adam and Eve had the shortest roots of anyone. The carefully narrated roots of the children of Israel take up a significant portion of the Old Testament. The genealogy of Jesus is spelled out by both Matthew and Luke. John the Revelator describes God's record book, which will be opened at the end of time. But nowhere in Scripture is there a better account of instructions from God on a memorial designed to teach coming generations their roots than this paragraph from Joshua.

"When your children shall ask their fathers in time to come, saying, What mean these stones? Then ye shall let your children know, saying, Israel came over this Jordan on dry land" (Josh. 4:21-22).

When parents teach children their roots, several hidden shoots need to be uncovered and examined:

The heroes of the past: It would be difficult for any father or mother to talk about the memorial at Gilgal without praising the exploits of Joshua; his partner, Caleb; and their predecessor, Moses. What child among the Israelite children would fail to get inspired talking about the heroes of their extended family?

Important times and places: Gilgal and the Jordan River, just after the time of Moses' death, when Joshua became the new leader, was a time and place that rivaled the Exodus from Egypt and the delivery of the commandments on Sinai. It held historic importance for the children of all Israelite parents. Every child in every cultural heritage deserves to know the significant dates and places in his roots. If he does not, his life has been robbed of a fulfilling dimension. In spite of existentialism, history still holds compelling importance.

Recognition of Providence: "For the Lord your God dried up the waters of Jordan . . . as the Lord your God did to the Red sea . . . that all the people . . . might know the hand of the Lord," Joshua reminded them (Josh. 4:23-24). The ultimate purpose for knowing our roots is to appreciate more fully the hand of God in our behalf. None of us would be alive if it were not for the miraculous moments of intervention when forefathers and mothers were spared and their lives saved. All of this is that we "might know the hand of the Lord, that it is mighty: that [we] might fear [respect] the Lord [our] God for ever."

Parents as Teachers

Every baby is born with two fears: falling (losing support) and loud noises. Almost everything else a child knows is a

113

learned response. The mind of a child is much like a blank sheet of paper used to transmit a picture across the country. At first the sheet is empty, and then thousands of little printer's dots begin to appear on the empty sheet. In a matter of moments, the sheet becomes filled with the dots that form the picture; for instance, the image of the president in front of the White House.

Learning during the first dozen years of a child's life is much like that. During these years the child fills in the dots that answer for him one of the most important questions in life: What kind of a person am I?

What a mother teaches a child about himself during the first few years of life will likely not be undone later. Abraham Lincoln learned from his mother, "I am honest." His mother died when her boy Abe was only nine years old. But throughout his adult life, her son was known as "Honest Abe." The "unfeigned faith" Paul saw in Timothy, he also saw in his mother, Eunice, and his grandmother, Lois.

Grandmothers are almost always more traditional than their daughters. This conservatism is often a good balance to the more open ways of the younger generation. Grandmothers have more time and are often more loving than their sons and daughters. A good grandmother is often more objective about a grandson than his mother and can be a wonderful counselor. Timothy was fortunate to be reared under the watchful, loving eye of a good grandmother.

Then, Timothy had a father figure, Paul. Every child needs the influence of a good, emotionally stable man. Since nothing is said concerning a husband of Eunice or Lois, it is likely the two women were widows. If this is true, Timothy was a fortunate young man to have received the attention of Paul, (1) who saw him as a "dearly beloved son," (2) for whom "without ceasing" he had "remembrance" in his "prayers night and day." Furthermore, (3) Paul desired greatly to see Timothy, that he might be filled with joy. Not every boy has a father. And not every boy who has a father learns from him to "thank God," whom Paul served from his "forefathers with pure conscience." In every child's life there needs to be a man of integrity and faith who can transmit these qualities to his child.

Curriculum

We are not without guidance on the curriculum parents need for teaching their children. The wind that bends the twig that forms the shape of the tree comes from the hearth of home and not from the teacher's whistle in the school yard. There is a universal home study course that needs to include several important elements.

First, there is subject matter to be learned: "But continue thou in the things which thou hast learned," Paul advises. The four Rs of children's learning are still basic: *(a)* reading, *(b)* 'riting, *(c)* 'rithmetic, and *(d)* religion. Even though these ideas can be taught outside the home, the attitude and level of encouragement and climate for learning within the home will be a determining factor in what, how much, and how well these things will be learned.

Then, there are assurances every child needs to receive: "But continue thou in the things which thou . . . hast been assured of." Webster says an assurance is "a declaration tending to inspire full confidence." There are some assurances every child needs to receive in the home: *(a)* he needs to be assured of "grace, mercy, and peace" that come from God the Father, who is a loving person like Jesus Christ our Lord. *(b)* He needs to be assured that he is loved and accepted unconditionally by his parents just because they belong to each other. *(c)* He needs to be assured of his own unique value as a person who is worthwhile.

Third, there are persons to be remembered and respected: "But continue thou in the things which thou hast learned . . . knowing of whom thou hast learned them." If parents depreciate (put down) authority and authority figures, children will do the same. If parents show respect for each other, children will tend to learn the same respect. Parents who allow their children to grow up without learning respect have not done them a favor.

Above all, the Bible is a book to be learned and lived: I have often asked myself what a child should know who has attended Sunday School on a regular basis for the first 12 years of his life. There are many things he might learn, such as churchmanship, Christian fellowship, Christian love, and the goodness of God. However, the one thing the child should know after systematic involvement in church for a dozen years is knowledge and respect for the contents of the Bible. Timothy, from a child, knew the Holy Scriptures.

Finally, a child needs to be taught the meaning of salvation: Paul reminds parents that it is the Holy Scriptures that make their children "wise unto salvation through faith which is in Christ Jesus." What greater joy is there for parents than to lead their child into the experience of the new birth in Christ Jesus. The evangelist, pastor, Sunday School teacher, or church worker may lead a child to know Christ, but the most logical person to lead a child to become Christian is the Christian father and/or mother of the child.

Chapter 11

When Families Self-destruct

Scriptural Stepping-stones

"Where your treasure is"

> "Lay not up for yourselves treasures upon earth, where moth and rust doth corrupt, and where thieves break through and steal: but *lay up for yourselves treasures in heaven, where neither moth nor rust doth corrupt, and where thieves do not break through nor steal: for where your treasure is, there will your heart be also.*"
>
> Matt. 6:19-21

* * *

"No man can serve two masters"

> "The light of the body is the eye: if therefore thine eye be single, thy whole body shall be full of light. But if thine eye be evil, thy whole body shall be full of darkness. If therefore the light that is in thee be darkness, how great is that darkness! *No man can serve two masters: for either he will hate the one, and love the other; or else he will hold to the one, and despise the other.* Ye cannot serve God and mammon."
>
> Matt. 6:22-24

* * *

"Solomon in all his glory . . ."

"Therefore I say unto you, *Take no thought for* your life, *what ye shall eat,* or *what ye shall drink;* nor yet for your body, *what ye shall put on.* Is not the life more than meat, and the body than raiment? Behold the fowls of the air: for they sow not, neither do they reap, nor gather into barns; yet your heavenly Father feedeth them. Are ye not much better than they? *Which of you by taking thought can add one cubit unto his stature?* And why take ye thought for raiment? Consider the lilies of the field, how they grow; they toil not, neither do they spin: and yet I say unto you, That even Solomon in all his glory was not arrayed like one of these. Wherefore, if God so clothe the grass of the field, which to day is, and to morrow is cast into the oven, shall he not much more clothe you, O ye of little faith? Therefore take no thought, saying, What shall we eat? or, What shall we drink? or, Wherewithall shall we be clothed? (For after all these things do the Gentiles seek:) for your heavenly Father knoweth that ye have need of all these things. *But seek ye first the kingdom of God, and his righteousness; and all these things shall be added unto you.* Take therefore no thought for the morrow: for the morrow shall take thought for the things of itself. Sufficient unto the day is the evil thereof."

Matt. 6:25-34

Stress is blamed for many of the ills that have fallen on modern man, including physical sickness and family breakdowns. And pressure is to stress what boiling water is to a tea kettle. Pressure comes from the frustrating experiences of life. When the snows in the Cascade Mountains of Oregon melt into the creek beds and rivers that empty into the Columbia

River gorge, a great wall of water flows in one mighty surge toward the Pacific Ocean until it hits the Bonneville Dam some 35 miles out of Portland. Frustrated or blocked by the impenetrable wall of concrete and steel, the water begins to back up and rise higher until the pressure per cubic inch on the great dam is unimaginable in human terms. Unless the spillway is opened to relieve this pressure, it will continue to build until it finds its own outlet by bursting the dam or going around it. In either case, there is death and destruction in the gorge as the water rolls over whatever gets in its way.

This analogy of the dam and the pressures that build up against modern families has in it a number of practical lessons. (1) Pressure is a fact of life in every household. It expresses itself in many ways, including heightened irritability, accident proneness, apathy, headaches, and even tantrums. (2) No family can take an infinite amount of pressure. Eventually, something has to give. When the pressure becomes too great, there are only two options: *(a)* Increase the family's tolerance for stress, or *(b)* decrease the stress. Since it is difficult to increase stress tolerance, disruptive action is often the alternative. (3) In families unable to cope with the pressures of the world there are several unsatisfactory responses: *(a)* There can be physical and emotional illnesses, including a nervous breakdown. *(b)* Various modes of escape, including alcoholism and drug addiction, may develop from within a family. *(c)* There can even be physical violence. *(d)* There may be breakup of the family by divorce or desertion. *(e)* And there may be an ethical breakdown that leads to various forms of dishonesty.

These directives from the heart of Jesus' teachings in the Sermon on the Mount point to four of the most common kinds of family pressure: (1) money and possessions, (2) distorted values, (3) split loyalties, and (4) unwarranted worry. These can become the source of great pressure and stress, which lead the marriage to self-destruct.

Money and Possessions

The pressures for more money and for buying and gathering more possessions are unrelenting in the average home. Jesus declared, "Where your treasure is, there will your heart be also" (Matt. 6:21). The family whose major focus is on materialism, whether it be for survival or self-aggrandizement, pays a surcharge that taxes the capacity of the family to cope.

Most families have no foolproof hedge against double-digit inflation and double-digit unemployment in the same year. People on fixed incomes can be devastated by demands completely beyond their control. Young couples trying to buy their first house at today's prices are under increased pressure with each other by their commitment to make paypayments that stretch their financial reach. These problems and many more are related to the pressures every family feels on money and possessions. Buying groceries can be a center of contention. If Jesus were here on earth in person today, what would He have to say on the subject of money and earthly possessions? His figures of speech might be different, but His understanding would be the same. Here are some suggestions that fit the tenor of discussions He had with His disciples in Galilee.

Job skills can become worthless: Even the basic skills of a family provider can be destroyed or obliterated by automation at an age in the worker's life span when learning a new trade is hard and maybe impossible. If your security is only in your own job skills, your treasure can turn to ashes in your hands.

Treasures can be destroyed: In the ancient world a man's wardrobe was considered part of his net worth because of the great expense of woven cloth, particularly dyed cloth. Purple cloth was considered to be of higher value because of the rare dye used in making it. But one moth in a bolt of cloth or an expensive purple robe could shortly destroy its value.

Treasures can be corroded: In the ancient world, there were two ways rust corrupted values. (1) Metals were of high value because they were scarce. Brass, particularly, was subject to both corrosion and erosion. (2) Corn and grain, which had to be stored for future needs, was always subject to the destruction of time, weather, and rodents. If woven cloth was subject to moths, then metals and granaries were even more subject to rust. There is no foolproof way to lay up these treasures on earth.

Some treasures can be stolen: Bands of roving thieves made highways treacherous in the ancient world. And baked clay construction in ordinary homes made it easy for thieves to break through walls and floors to steal.

The basic lesson of Jesus on money and possessions is still operative today. The more dependent a family is on money and possessions for happiness, the more subject they are to problems beyond their control, since the value of things rises and falls, and no one can predict or control these changes in values.

Distorted Values

The most humble amateur photographer knows that no picture ever looks good unless the focus is accurate and the amount of light through the lens is proper. The camera industry has spent millions of dollars in research to make the light and the focusing devices accurate for millions of part-time photographers. Even the amateur picture taker wants assurance his shots are on target. The inner spirit of man, which serves as the retina of his life, needs accurate focus and proper light to get good views of what is going on in the world. Errors in focusing and shading of light can cause a man to have distorted views of what is going on around him.

The eyes are the camera of the body: "The light of the body is the eye" (Matt. 6:22). Too little light into the eyes, or too much light onto the sensitive retina causes blindness. If the family is blind to the world and what it is doing to them, the predictable result is confusion, hurt feelings, and multiple accidents in family relationships. Little things are blown out of proportion, and important matters are obscured.

The eyes can distort a person's sense of values: "If therefore thine eye be single, thy whole body shall be full of light" (Matt. 6:22). No one knows better than the merchandisers and advertising agencies how to distort vision and confuse a family's sense of values. The most popular distorters of family values are well known: (1) *Distorted use of television viewing* can kill family conversation, feed the family a celluloid diet of sex and violence, give children a wrong sense of priorities, and provide a popular brand of religion without Christian commitment or discipline. (2) *An overemphasis on athletics* impacts values for the home. Athletic contests are important, but not all-important. Football may be big business, but it is still only a game. (3) *Consumer debt* has risen to frightening heights in many families. Impulse buying and emotional decisions to purchase by payment plans has caused many to feel that they can buy more than what they are really able to pay for. The ultimate result is more pressure and stress in the home. (4) *Making money at any cost* to the detriment of the physical and emotional health of the family is too big a price to pay for material gain.

Uncertain Loyalties

In the ancient world, masters had slaves, not employees. There was no middle class, no union, and no government agency to guard the interests of the unprotected. There were just free men and slaves. Slaves were merchandise, a part of man's net worth. Slaves could be bought, sold, traded, or used for collateral in a loan. A slave could not vote or own property. In fact, a slave had no time of his own. He was on call 24 hours a day, seven days a week. His obligation to his master was complete. He could not be owned by two men because it was impossible to serve two masters.

Many families are confused and in disarray because they have not yet decided who owns them. (1) "No man can serve two masters." There is a reason for this. Divided loyalties are fickle. "Either he will hate the one, and love the other; or else he will hold to the one, and despise the other." Everyone finally has only one master; he cannot have two. (2) "Ye cannot serve God and mammon," Jesus stated. There is a practical sense in which attention must be given to making a living, keeping the house, cooking the meals, and all else that takes care of the physical needs of the family. Failure to meet these obligations becomes legal neglect, and someone is answerable to law. But beyond the practical application of the prudent man or woman in necessary earthly affairs, each one of us is finally dominated by the spiritual and moral values of life or by the worldly possessions in which we invested our trust. We can't have it both ways.

For the Christian who wants to be dominated by spiritual and moral values and not by possessions, there are three guidelines: (1) At best, we are only stewards. God created everything, and therefore everything belongs to Him. "The earth is the Lord's, and the fulness thereof; the world, and they that dwell therein" (Ps. 24:1). (2) No physical possession is more important than the persons related to it. If a businessman sacrifices his children for his fortune, they have both been exploited. Can you imagine Christ destroying a man and his business to make it His own? With Christ people came first. Jesus turned water to wine, but He never turned people into merchandise. (3) Regardless of the priority of wealth in a capitalistic society, possessions after a certain minimal level of survival are secondary to other greater values. It is the love of money and not money itself that is the root of evil. It is a grave responsibility to have more possessions than you can handle. And it is self-destructive to be dominated by things.

Wasted Worry

The disproportionate amount of space Jesus gave to worry indicates how widespread this problem was then and is now. Jesus spelled out three areas of unwarranted worry that still exist in modern families.

126

There is unwarranted worry about life-style: Jesus directed, "Take no thought for your life, what ye shall eat ... drink ... put on." For most families, food is not a matter of life or death; it is a matter of style. Most families are concerned more about the style with which they eat and drink, and the clothes they put on, than they are about minimal intake and covering their nakedness against heat or cold. This concern includes (1) the restaurants they frequently visit, (2) the home, apartment, or condominium where they live, (3) the cars they drive, (4) the clothes they wear, and (5) the recreation and vacations they enjoy. All of these factors in life-styles are important but not worth unwarranted worry.

Unwarranted worry over status: "Which of you by taking thought can add one cubit unto his stature?" is our Lord's next question. Since a cubit is 18 inches or roughly the distance from a man's elbow to the tip of his fingers, it is not likely Jesus was using the cubit in a literal sense. Most people would look deformed if they were suddenly 18 inches taller. It is much more likely that Jesus was talking about the level of status or importance a person has in his own little world.

Unwarranted worry about tomorrow: There is a prudent level of concern for tomorrow. We had better worry about the durability of the roof on our house, the education of our children, retirement income, and the probable results of our health habits. But there are some things worry won't change. (1) Aging and death will not be altered or postponed by unwarranted worry. (2) All the worry in the world will not stop the winter cold, the summer heat, or the coming of floods, tornadoes, hurricanes, and earthquakes. (3) Worrying over grown children will neither protect nor change them. In short, it is foolish to worry about things beyond our control.

Chapter 12

Single Person Households

Scriptural Stepping-stones

"Martha received him into her house"

> "Now it came to pass, as they went, that he entered into a certain village: and *a certain woman named Martha received him into her house. And she had a sister called Mary,* which also sat at Jesus' feet, and heard his word. But Martha was cumbered about much serving, and came to him, and said, Lord, dost thou not care that my sister hath left me to serve alone? bid her therefore that she help me. And Jesus answered and said unto her, *Martha, Martha, thou art careful and troubled about many things:* but one thing is needful: and Mary hath chosen that good part, which shall not be taken away from her."
>
> Luke 10:38-42

*   *   *

"To the unmarried and widows"

> "For I would that all men were even as I myself. But *every man hath his proper gift of God, one after this manner, and another after that.* I say therefore to the unmarried and widows, It is good for them if they abide even as I. But if they cannot contain, let them marry: for it is better to marry than to burn."
>
> 1 Cor. 7:7-9

"Now concerning virgins"

"Now concerning virgins, *I have no commandment of the Lord: yet I give my judgment,* as one that hath obtained mercy of the Lord to be faithful. I suppose therefore that this is good for the present distress, I say, that it is good for a man so to be. Art thou bound unto a wife? seek not to be loosed. Art thou loosed from a wife? seek not a wife. But and if thou marry, thou hast not sinned; and if a virgin marry, she hath not sinned. Nevertheless such shall have trouble in the flesh: but I spare you."

1 Cor. 7:25-28

* * *

"There is difference"

"But I would have you without carefulness. *He that is unmarried careth for the things that belong to the Lord,* how he may please the Lord: but *he that is married careth* for the things that are of the world, *how he may please his wife. There is difference* also between a wife and a virgin. *The unmarried woman careth for the things of the Lord,* that she may be holy both in body and in spirit: but *she that is married careth* for the things of the world, *how she may please her husband.*"

1 Cor. 7:32-34

Dating for most people soon leads to marriage. In the United States, 93 percent of the women and 92 percent of the men over 45 years of age are married or have been. However, there is a proportion of the population who never marry and another proportion who have been married, but then by death or divorce become single again.

From a numerical perspective, most people who desire marriage should be able to find a mate. (1) Under age 20, there are more men than women. (2) From 20 to 24 the number of both men and women is about equal. (3) After 24 there are more women than men in the population.

However, other factors complicate the balance of marriageable people: (1) There are more men than women who are not marriageable for mental, emotional, and physical reasons. (2) Men tend to marry women who are younger than themselves. The average man of 35 marries a woman 6½ years younger than himself, and there are more women in the age-group from 25 to 29 than there are men in the age-group of 30-34. (3) Furthermore, there are more single women working in cities than single men. It has been estimated that living in cities lowers the percentage of married people by 10 percent, which means that 10 percent more people of comparable age would be married if they lived in the country and small towns.

In *Building a Successful Marriage,* by Landis and Landis, from which the above data is taken, the authors write, "Because most people do marry, the single person is usually aware of a strong pressure toward conformity" (p. 85). This pressure had some negative consequences: (1) Some people marry before they are emotionally ready and before they are mature enough to handle the adjustment problems of marriage and are able to face the financial demands marriage makes. (2) Others feel pressure to marry when the available mate, by the standards of family and friends, is unsuitable. This kind of marriage can result in legal divorce, or even in psychological divorce in which the marriage is never satisfactory.

131

Many people who marry under the pressure of the social system might remain single if the expectation of the culture were different. (1) Many disastrous marriages would be prevented. (2) Without doubt, the age of marriage would rise. (3) The obsessive compulsion to marry would be reduced.

But consciously or unconsciously, there is a norm in the culture that all but demands marriage as a badge of normalcy; and those who don't marry need to feel for themselves, "I could have." And to this their friends answer, "Why didn't you?" In a sense these questions are legitimate, because God organized the human race into families and instructed the first parents to multiply and replenish the earth. But the circumstances of life for individual cases alter the ideal, and as a result many people live part or all of their life as a single person.

There are acceptable Christian life-styles for single people. In the scripture passages chosen for this study there are several categories of unmarried people. There are (1) the unmarried, (2) those who have been married and are now single, (3) the virgins, both men and women who have not consummated a marriage. And finally, there is a defense of unmarried people whose focus of attention is on spiritual matters.

Single Women by Choice?

Research has for many years concentrated on the challenges, problems, and satisfactions of marriage, while singleness as a life-style has been subject to folklore, hearsay, and even derisive humor. It takes strength just to withstand these pressures without developing visible defense mechanisms.

But regardless of the reasons, a person should be allowed to remain single by choice with no social stigma. Some remain single because they are more autonomous persons than others. They are self-directed and have goals with clear meanings. It is easy to see this pattern in Martha and Mary. (1) They were mature ladies. *(a)* They had their own house. *(b)* No reference is made to parents or relatives on whom they depended emotionally or financially. *(c)* They had extra space to keep Jesus and apparently had the kind of home where He could feel comfortable. (2) They were autonomous. Not only were they independent as sisters, but they were autonomous as persons. Each had her distinctive personality that made her an individual. *(a)* Martha was a compulsive doer, a perfectionist housekeeper, and a great hostess. *(b)* Mary was contemplative, given to stimulating conversation, and somewhat aloof from the feeling of the responsibilities of cooking and hosting. *(c)* Martha was probably a perfectionist by nature, "careful and troubled about many things," while Mary had chosen the "one thing [that] is needful."

We may like Martha more than Mary, or Mary more than Martha. It does not matter. The point is that they were two mature women living together, autonomous and independent by nature, who had the kind of home where Jesus felt comfortable.

Married Once and Single Again

We have noted the role of men and women who have been married and then by death or desertion have passed through the married state into singleness and the more mature years. Consider:

Paul was a single person: The apostle wrote, "I would that all men were even as I myself." There has been much discussion on the bachelor state and life-style of Paul. William Barclay declares, "We may be fairly certain that at some time Paul had been married" (*The Letters to the Corinthians,* in *Daily Study Bible,* p. 60). Barclay's conclusion comes from the following lines of evidence. (1) Paul was a rabbi who claimed never to have failed in the strictest requirements of tradition. Orthodox Jews believed in marriage as an obligation. Failure to marry was failure to fulfill the commandment of God on bearing children in order to replenish the earth. Since 18 was the age for a man to marry, Barclay believes "it is in the highest degree unlikely that so devout and orthodox a Jew as Paul was would have remained unmarried" (p. 61). Also (2) Paul was a member of the Sanhedrin (Acts 26:10), and marriage was a requirement for membership since "it was held that married men were more merciful" (p. 61).

Some think Paul's wife may well have left him when he became a Christian. Or she may have died early in their marriage. In either case, Paul seems to have turned his back on marriage and family in favor of a very intense life of Christian service. Because of the seriousness of the times and the great need for evangelization, Paul seems to have disparaged marriage for others as well as himself.

Paul's advice on singleness was to others as well as for himself: "To the unmarried and widows, It is good for them if they abide even as I," he recommended. There are several disadvantages in being single. (1) Loneliness is probably the biggest problem. Many pleasant activities, such as travel, are less fulfilling when experienced alone. However, people can be married and still be lonely. (2) Most kinds of social life are

134

organized on the basis of couples and families. (3) There is the embarrassment resulting from the matchmaking efforts of friends and family. (4) Some degree of sexual deprivation and frustration is likely to be experienced by the unmarried, especially the intimate closeness of being loved and accepted unconditionally by someone who makes your life count. (5) Some unmarried persons regret that they have never had children of their very own. (6) And some unmarried persons suffer from the lack of an exclusive relationship that provides emotional security. Rollo May, Smiley Blanton, and other psychiatrists say that married people live longer than singles. This fact may be an indication of the importance of meeting the human need for emotional closeness provided in marriage.

But there are advantages in being single that cannot be ignored. (1) Single living makes less demands on the time and energy of the individual than marriage and family. Single people have more discretionary time than most married people. Cooperative living doesn't come easy for all husbands and wives. (2) There are financial advantages with some singles, since two cannot live as cheaply as one. (3) Since the single person is responsible only to himself—or herself—the control of one's life is much more direct, including both short-range and long-range plans. (4) In cases where the widowed or divorced person has thoughts dominated by memories from former years in a stressful marriage, even loneliness can be bearable.

Virgins

Choosing a life of celibacy is a matter of personal judgment: "I give my judgment," the apostle puts it, identifying his remarks on celibacy as personal opinion. If every marriageable adult chose a celibate life-style, the population growth would go to zero in one generation and ultimately delete the human race. But for those who choose the celibate option, it is a matter of personal judgment, which has advantages and disadvantages.

Those who are married should enjoy the relationship: Paul says, "But and if thou marry, thou hast not sinned; and if a virgin marry, she hath not sinned" (v. 28). There is nothing evil about a husband and wife living as a husband and wife.

Singles and Christian Service

Paul believed there were advantages in Christian service for those who were not married.

Marriage brings added responsibilities. In marriage, both the husband and wife are preoccupied with their obligations to each other. (1) Paul would have had great difficulty keeping his far-flung travel schedule if he had been married. It would have been unfair to his wife. (2) Paul might never have had the time to be so productive as a minister of Christ if he had been married. He wrote one-quarter of the New Testament and directly influenced Luke, who wrote another quarter of it. He was an evangelist, missionary, theologian, and church administrator. For 10 years he served as superintendent of the Aegean District with churches in both Turkey and Asia Minor, and congregations in such places as Ephesus, Corinth, and Thessalonica. Being unattached and unencumbered may have been important to Paul's productivity. (3) The sublimation of sexual energy into constructive work has long been recognized by students of human nature as a source of creativity. Many great poets, painters, writers, and administrators have been single. Even many creative persons who have been married, such as Lincoln, Jefferson, and Wesley, had less than successful marriage relationships.

All of this means that God can use single people in wonderful ways that are creative and productive. Therefore, let us love, accept, and support our single brothers and sisters in the Lord, because our Heavenly Father may have a very special ministry for them.

Chapter *13*

Nurturing the Next Generation

Scriptural Stepping-stones

"Love the Lord thy God"

> "Hear, O Israel: *The Lord our God is one Lord:* and thou shalt *love the Lord thy God with all thine heart,* and with all thy *soul,* and with all thy *might.*"
>
> Deut. 6:4-5

*   *   *

"These words . . . shall be in thy heart"

> "And these words, which I command thee this day, shall be in thine heart: and thou shalt *teach them diligently unto thy children,* and shalt *talk of them when thou sittest* in thine house, and *when thou walkest* by the way, and *when thou liest down,* and *when thou risest up.* And thou shalt bind them for a sign upon thine hand, and they shall be as frontlets between thine eyes. And thou shalt *write them* upon the posts of thy house, and on thy gates."
>
> Deut. 6:6-9

*   *   *

"And when thy son asketh thee"

> "And thou shalt do that which is right and good in the sight of the Lord: that it may be well with thee, and that thou mayest go in and possess the good land which the

139

Lord sware unto thy fathers, to cast out all thine enemies from before thee, as the Lord hath spoken. And *when thy son asketh thee* in time to come, saying, *what mean the testimonies, and the statutes, and the judgments,* which the Lord our God hath commanded you? Then thou shalt say unto thy son, We were Pharaoh's bondmen in Egypt; and the Lord brought us out of Egypt with a mighty hand: and the Lord shewed signs and wonders, great and sore, upon Egypt, upon Pharaoh, and upon all his household, before our eyes: and he brought us out from thence, that he might bring us in, to give us the land which he sware unto our fathers. And the Lord commanded us to do all these statutes, to fear the Lord our God, for our good always, that he might preserve us alive, as it is at this day. And it shall be our righteousness, if we observe to do all these commandments before the Lord our God, as he hath commanded us."

Deut. 6:18-25

Within the teaching/learning process of the children of God, Deuteronomy stands in a special place. (1) Genesis is the book of beginnings about the children of God becoming a nation. (2) Exodus is the story of the departure from Egypt and the welding of the people into a strong nation by the establishing of the law and the principle of obedience to God. (3) Leviticus is a book on how the people were to worship. (4) Numbers is the story of the wilderness wanderings. And (5) Deuteronomy relates to the final preparations for Israel's entering the Promised Land.

Deuteronomy is the second declaration of the law, but not a repetition of it. This book contains the addresses of Moses at very strategic times: (1) just before he died on Pisgah,

(2) at the very end of the wandering, (3) at the time for the conquest of Canaan by Israel, and (4) at the time when a new leader, Joshua, was assuming his authority.

Every family of Christians is just one generation away from spiritual extinction. The living faith is not transmitted through the genes. It is taught and accepted by each new generation. The generation of Israelites who wandered in the desert 40 years were almost gone. (1) They were there when God opened up the Red Sea and let them pass on dry ground. (2) They were there when Moses came down out of Sinai with the commandments. (3) They had seen the glory of God in the pillar of cloud by day and the pillar of fire by night. But it was now time to teach the children and young people the truth about a living faith. The faith of their fathers must become their own.

The Central Lesson

Deut. 6:4-9 is one of the most important passages on the family in the Bible, judged both by its content and by the scope of its influence on (1) Judaism, (2) Jesus, and (3) the Church. The first word, "Hear," constitutes the title of the passage for the Jews, who call it "Shema," the Hebrew word for "hear." For more than 3,000 years, loyal Jews have been reciting these verses twice daily. Jesus united Deut. 6:4-5 with Lev. 19:18 for His definitive proclamation that answered the question, "Which is the first commandment?" When queried on the greatest commandment, Jesus responded with this statement from Moses: "Hear, O Israel; The Lord our God is one Lord: and thou shalt love the Lord thy God with all thy heart, and with all thy soul, and with all thy mind, and with all

141

thy strength . . . Thou shalt love thy neighbour as thyself. There is none other commandment greater than these" (Mark 12:29-31). For nearly 2,000 years, Christians have been quoting this statement from Jesus' summary of the law.

First, there is the uncomplicated simplicity of the command: "The Lord our God is one Lord" (v. 4). All through their history, the children of Israel were surrounded by people who believed in many gods. This was true in Egypt, in the Sinai desert, and during the conquest by Israel. This is why the one important basic lesson the children learned from Moses was, "The Lord our God is one Lord."

If every child could learn to believe in one God, one Lord, everything else they learn could fall into place. (1) In the beginning God made the world. (2) When man came to be, it was God who made him. (3) From all people, God selected Abraham to father a nation who would live in a special relationship with Him. (4) Since Jesus, who was a member of that chosen nation, became the Human Being in whom God came down to dwell fully, then Jesus Christ was a unique person, the God-man, God's only Son. (5) In a mysterious way beyond human explanation Jesus Christ gave himself for us on a cross that the internal battle against sin in us may be won and that we may live in full fellowship with God through acceptance of Jesus Christ as Savior. (6) The source of strength for living the fulfilled life on earth is the presence of the indwelling Christ. However, if we do not begin with God our Lord who is one God, there is no theology of redemption and no living faith to propel us through the spaces of an uncharted life.

And second, belief in one God can be demonstrated: "And thou shalt love the Lord thy God." To fear God, or run from

142

God, may be understood from the nature of man's heart as displayed in the disobedience of Adam and Eve and all their descendants. "The heart is deceitful above all things, and desperately wicked: who can know it? I the Lord search the heart" (Jer. 17:9-10). Some form of the word "deceive" is used more than 150 times in the Bible. The antidote to fear and deception is love.

Hosea was the first to use "love" in a religious sense—God loved Israel (Hos. 3:1; 9:15; 11:1, 4; 14:4). But the earliest use of the word "love" as man's response to God is in Deuteronomy. Moses said it again and again, that God basically wanted the people of Israel to be loyal and obedient in their love to Him (5:10; 7:9; 11:1; 13:3; and 19:9). If we love God fully, it becomes much easier to (1) love our neighbor, and then to (2) love ourselves.

What Makes a Good Teacher at Home?

How to teach children is a full-blown area of research involving huge sums of money and the skills of some of the most scholarly men of every generation, including such greats as Rousseau and John Dewey. But every great leader is a teacher by the very nature of leadership. Jesus was the greatest Teacher of all. And Moses was a strong second. What makes a mother or father a good teacher?

Credibility: The only credible teacher is the one who believes in what is being taught. "And these words, which I command thee this day, shall be in thine heart" (v. 6). The teacher who does not love God can teach about the love of God and raise searching questions about the meaning of love. But the

143

only teacher who can teach children to love God must be fully in love with Him himself.

Diligence: The teacher needs to be enthusiastic. "And thou shalt teach them diligently unto thy children" (v. 7). Nurture is caught as much as it is taught. My advisor at Michigan State University often chose my graduate courses on the basis of who taught them instead of the subject being taught. A great teacher will inspire students to learn, while dull teachers will turn them off.

Interest: Learning begins only when discussion is generated. "Talk of them when thou sittest in thine house, and when thou walkest by the way, and when thou liest down, and when thou risest up" (v. 7). Max Lerner, columnist and teacher, believes no learning really takes place until the teaching in the classroom generates discussion in the street and at home. Sermons that do not generate wholesome discussion at the Sunday dinner table are not remembered. Either the preacher/teacher did not come across as convinced of what he was saying, or he was dull and uninteresting. When Phillips Brooks was asked why his church, which seated only 400 people, made such an impact on Boston, he answered that it was because 400 people were repreaching his sermon all week long.

Reiteration: Truth must be kept before our eyes. "And thou shalt bind them for a sign upon thine hand, and they shall be as frontlets between thine eyes. And thou shalt write them upon the posts of thy house, and on thy gates" (vv. 8-9).

The word to bind the commands on the hand, to wear them on the forehead, and to write them on the doorposts may originally have been meant figuratively. The *New Inter-*

national Version reads, "It will be like a sign on your hand and a symbol on your forehead that the Lord brought us out of Egypt with his mighty hand" (Exod. 13:16). But some Jews from before the time of Jesus to now have followed the command literally. They inscribe Exod. 13:1-10 and 11-16 and Deut. 6:4-9 and 11:13-21 on tiny scrolls of parchment, insert them in cases of skin or metal, and bind them on the arm and on the forehead at the time of reciting the Shema. In addition, they prepare a small cylinder enclosing Deut. 6:4-9 and 11:13-21 to the upper part of the right doorpost. The "phylacteries" of Matt. 23:5 are the cases worn on the arm and the forehead.

The Rewards of Teaching

There are always dangers in receiving God's blessings. (1) Moses was afraid material abundance in a growing nation might dull the people's awareness of God and the memory of the pit from which they had been dug (Deut. 6:10-12). (2) Moses was afraid the success of the children of Israel might make it easy to join their pagan neighbors in worshiping multiple gods as an addendum to their worship of Jehovah. Moses reminded the people that the Lord is a "jealous" God (v. 15). And finally, Moses was afraid (3) the people might question the providence of God and feel that the Lord had deserted them when things got difficult (9:22; 33:8).

The last paragraph in chapter 11 is not concerned with the people entering Canaan but with their descendants—"that your days may be multiplied, and the days of your children" (v. 21).

145

There are four ways to prove our love to God: "For if ye shall diligently keep all these commandments . . . to do them, to love the Lord your God, to walk in all his ways, and to cleave unto him" (11:22), our love will be true.

"To do them." Our daily life-style, our decisions, and our behavior are the means by which we "do" the commandments.

"To love the Lord." Love is *(a)* a way of seeing a person, *(b)* an emotion toward a person, *(c)* a commitment to a person, and *(d)* a relationship with a person.

"To walk in all his ways." The New Testament says much more about walking than running. Most of our life in Him is a walk and not a race, a cross-country journey and not a 100-yard dash.

"To cleave unto him." God said a man is to leave his own father and mother and cleave to his wife. This does not mean a man must despise his parents in order to love his wife. But it does mean that under God she is the central focus of his attention and the first priority in his decisions. Hence, a Christian does not despise his family and friends to prove his love for God. He just makes God the central Focus of his life and the first priority in his decisions.

And there are promises and rewards for the faithful: Moses promises, "Then will the Lord . . ." If one goalpost is the big "if," the other is the big "then"—the promises will follow. (1) You will be stronger than you ever thought you could be. "Then . . . ye shall possess greater nations and mightier than yourselves" (11:23). Many a Christian has experienced successes beyond himself because of faith in God. (2) Your goals will be reached. "Every place whereon the soles of your feet shall tread shall be yours" (v. 24). And (3) even your enemies cannot destroy you. "There shall no man be able to stand before you" (v. 25).

Chapter *14*

The Family Beyond the Family

Scriptural Stepping-stones

"Breaking bread from house to house"

"And they continued stedfastly in the apostles' doctrine and fellowship, and in breaking of bread, and in prayers. And fear came upon every soul: and many wonders and signs were done by the apostles. And all that believed were together, and had all things common; and sold their possessions and goods, and parted them to all men, as every man had need. *And they, continuing daily with one accord in the temple, and breaking bread from house to house, did eat their meat with gladness and singleness of heart, praising God, and having favour with all the people.* And the Lord added to the church daily such as should be saved."

Acts 2:42-47

*　*　*

"The fellowship"

"God is faithful, by whom *ye were called unto the fellowship* of his Son Jesus Christ our Lord."

1 Cor. 1:9

*　*　*

"That ye also may have fellowship"

> "That which was from the beginning, which we have heard, which we have seen with our eyes, which we have looked upon, and our hands have handled, of the word of life; (for the life was manifested, and we have seen it, and bear witness, and shew unto you that eternal life, which was with the Father, and was manifested unto us;) that which we have seen and heard declare we unto you, *that ye also may have fellowship with us:* and truly our fellowship is with the Father, and with his Son Jesus Christ. And these things write we unto you, *that your joy may be full.*"
>
> 1 John 1:1-4

Marriage is a symbol of the relationship between God the Father and His people. Isaiah saw God injured by a faithless deserter nation, like a wife who has been deserted by her husband, and vice versa. "For the Lord hath called thee as a woman forsaken and grieved in spirit" (Isa. 54:6). It must have been the thought of the beauty and liveliness of marriage, held together now with only a memory, that caused another prophet to say, "I remember thee, the kindness of thy youth, the love of thine espousals" (Jer. 2:2). The Book of Hosea reads like a parable of God's love for Israel as revealed in the love of a faithful husband to a wife who had prostituted herself in the marketplace.

New Testament writers saw Christians as members of the family of God. For them the fellowship of believers was the family of God. The Lord promises, "[I] will be a Father unto you, and ye shall be my sons and daughters" (2 Cor. 6:18). Paul further exhorts, "Husbands, love your wives, even as Christ also loved the church, and gave himself for it" (Eph.

150

5:25). This is why a man leaves his parents' home and is joined to his wife, and the two become one. In this important passage on home and family and the Church, Paul writes, "This is a great mystery: but I speak concerning Christ and the church" (v. 32). A clear picture of self-giving is seen in Christ as the Bridegroom who is willing to lay down His life for the Bride who is the Church.

The Family and the Family of God

There are several characteristics of life in the family that carry over into life in the family of God. Some are: study and learning, fellowship, prayer, devotion, reverence, sharing, self-giving, helping, supporting, and acceptance.

Study and learning: "And they continued stedfastly in the apostles' doctrine" (v. 42). Learning and transmitting the Christian faith is the combined responsibility of the family and the family of God. In the old days there was close connection between the home, the school, and the church. Now each functions separately on its own, except in those places where churches operate primary and secondary schools in co-operation with tuition-paying, and thus with vitally interested, parents. In many places the public school has ceased to be the ally of the church and often a weak partner of the home.

However, between the Christian home and the Christian Church there are strong ties. Both the Christian home and the Church teach the Bible as the Word of God. Both the Christian home and the Church are interested in spiritual strength for daily living. Both promote Christian morality and Christ-

151

like courtesy. Both function around the Christian ideal of love, as revealed in the expressions of joy, peace, long-suffering, gentleness, goodness, faith, meekness, and temperance (see Gal. 5:22-23).

Unless Christians in families and the church members in worship are learning and growing, the ideals of the family and the Church will be diminished. There is no growth without learning.

Fellowship and togetherness: "They continued stedfastly in . . . fellowship, and in breaking of bread" (v. 42). In the old days, fellowship in church was just an extension of fellowship in the home. Evenings of family fellowship in doing the dishes, working on school assignments, watching the open fire, counseling one another, enjoying the fine art of story-telling, living in an atmosphere of mutual trust, and listening to each other read the Bible aloud and pray, made for an easy transaction to the extended family in the church where the family's religious functions were carried on in an expanded way. In the extended family of the church there was mutual trust, supportiveness, counseling, edifying conversation, and a wider use of prayer and Bible reading as ways of drawing each other closer to one another and to God. To be part of a loving, caring, sharing fellowship is a religiously strengthening experience.

Prayer: "They continued stedfastly . . . in prayers" (v. 42). I once knew a colonel in Alaska who returned from the air-base to his home each noon for lunch and a prayer break. He called it his "pause that refreshes." Just as the colonel needed a prayer break each day, the family of God needs a prayer break each week—on Sunday. It probably is during the Sun-

152

day morning pastoral prayer that we most nearly fulfill the ideal of Jesus when He said that those who worship God must do so "in spirit and in truth" (John 4:24). There are three characteristics of prayer that make it the "pause that refreshes." (1) There is no spirit or truth without openness and honesty with ourselves and with others. (2) There is no openness and honesty unless there is spontaneity in our prayer, rather than clichés and worn-out phrases that have lost much of their meaning. (3) There is no spontaneity in prayer unless there has been closeness to God and to people. Prayer at its best in the family or the family of God comes from the overflow of a heart that has been warmed by the Spirit of God and kept open to the joys and sorrows of the people.

Mutual respect: "And fear came upon every soul" (v. 43). Fear as used here and many other places in the New Testament is not cringing, distrustful fright. Fear as used here is really "respect" or "awe." This means that in this family of God there was a general attitude of respect. We need respect for each other. We need respect for our parents, the pastor, and all other authority figures in our lives. We need respect for God. We need respect for time and what it does with problems in our lives. We need respect for ourselves. Until our self-image is strong enough to sustain us under pressure, life will always be threatening.

Spiritual action: "And many wonders and signs were done by the apostles" (v. 43). There are several kinds of miracles that happen in the family at home and among the extended family of God. The greatest miracle of all is the miracle of salvation. There are miracles of circumstances. Is your family mature enough to accept a closed door to be God's will as much as an open door? There are miracles of healing: of the body; of relationships; and of attitudes.

Mutuality: "And all that believed were together, and had all things common" (v. 44). "Middle-age mutuality" is a stage of marriage identified and described by marriage consultants. But persons in Christian families and those in the extended family of God do not need to wait for middle age to be in a fellowship of mutual support. Only legalists are nonsupportive of others in the wider church family. They enjoy calling attention to the shortcomings of fellow family members and are judgmental instead of edifying in their words of correction. But how enriching it is to be in a great family of Christian people who support each other, give each other the benefit of the doubt, and accept each other unconditionally, as Christ did us. Verses 44-45 show us that the Early Church was a sharing church.

Happiness: They "did eat their meat with gladness and singleness of heart" (v. 46). Abraham Lincoln asserted, "Every man is just about as happy as he chooses to be." The love and security of a home with prevailing happiness is worth more than money can buy. A church can be the happiest place a person ever goes outside his own home. At a Black church in a ghetto in the East, I was amazed how long the Sunday service continued. It went on for hours on end. "The reason for the long service," the pastor told me, "was that the church is the happiest place these people ever go. Their homes are dismal. They aren't anybody important on the job. But when they come to church they have recognition, acceptance, friendship, and a refurbishing of their battered egos by the Spirit of Christ. Theirs is a religion of the heart."

Jesus and the Family

Jesus understood all about family living. He was born into a family. His first 30 years were spent in close association with brothers and sisters. He knew the meaning of death in the family; many Bible scholars agree that Joseph may have died before Jesus came to maturity. He was very close to His mother, Mary. During those silent years before age 30, Jesus was learning all about family living.

But there came a time when relations with His own family members were strained to the breaking point. When He began His ministry, Mary took the older children with her and went to Capernaum to dissuade Him from His ministry and bring Him back home to run the carpenter shop. "Neither did his brethren believe in him" (John 7:5). It is no wonder He later declared, "A man's foes shall be they of his own household" (Matt. 10:36). And yet Jesus believed that marriage and family life were most sacred. Divorce can be legalized, rationalized, and normalized, but there still remains a strange immutability about the consummation of a marriage. And this is the way Jesus must feel about fellowship with those who are in the family of God.

Fellowship in the Family of God

Christian fellowship comes with eternal life: "And shew unto you that eternal life, which was with the Father, and was manifested unto us." Eternal life is not just living forever. If some people had to keep living forever just like they live now, it would be a dismal prospect. Eternal life is, first of all, a quality of life. In eternal life there is freedom from guilt, fear, and the need for revenge. There is freedom to love life, love people, and love God. There is joy in the prospect of each new day and faith enough to do you on a bad day. Eternal life is also fulfillment of life in the world to come.

Christian fellowship involves communion: "That ye also may have fellowship with us: and truly our fellowship is with the Father, and with his Son Jesus Christ." Communion is the intertwining of the spirits of two or more persons. Therefore there is a sense of close interaction among people who fight together in wars, suffer together in the same storm, or stick it out together in graduate school. Communion develops strong, prolonged, emotional ties among people of mutual concerns. This is why Christians in the extended family may have like minds and kindred spirits because of their love for God and His Son Jesus Christ and for each other.

Christian fellowship brings joy: "That your joy may be full." Joy is the Christian emotion. It is not pumped up or worked down. It is just there. Paul had joy when he wrote letters from a Roman jail. John was in the sunset years when he wrote this letter, but it is filled with joy. He was imprisoned on a little volcanic island, living in a cave when he wrote the Book of Revelation. Joy is not dependent on good health. Joy is not dependent on other people. Joy is not dependent on apparent success. Joy is a fruit of the Spirit that grows out of our love for God (Gal. 5:22).

Chapter 15

Stress in the Family

Scriptural Stepping-stones

"Obey your parents . . . for this is right"

> *"Children, obey your parents in the Lord: for this is right.*
> Honour thy father and mother; which is the first com-
> mandment with promise; that it may be well with thee,
> and thou mayest live long on the earth."
>
> Eph. 6:1-3

*   *   *

"Provoke not your children to wrath"

> "And, ye fathers, *provoke not your children to wrath:* but
> bring them up in the nurture and admonition of the
> Lord."
>
> Eph. 6:4

*   *   *

"Forgiving one another"

> "Put on therefore, as the elect of God, holy and beloved,
> bowels of mercies, kindness, humbleness of mind,
> meekness, longsuffering; *forbearing one another, and for-*
> *giving one another,* if any man have a quarrel against any:
> *even as Christ forgave you,* so also do ye. And above all

these things put on charity, which is the bond of perfectness."

Col. 3:12-14

*   *   *

"Teaching and admonishing one another"

"And let the peace of God rule in your hearts, to the which also ye are called in one body; and be ye thankful. Let the word of Christ dwell in you richly in all wisdom; *teaching and admonishing one another in psalms and hymns and spiritual songs, singing with grace in your hearts* to the Lord. And whatsoever ye do in word or deed, do all in the name of the Lord Jesus, giving thanks to God and the Father by him."

Col. 3:15-17

*   *   *

"Wives, submit . . . Husbands, love your wives"

"*Wives, submit yourselves unto your own husbands,* as it is fit in the Lord: *Husbands, love your wives, and be not bitter against them. Children, obey your parents* in all things: for this is well pleasing unto the Lord."

Col. 3:18-20

There are many Christian families who live together in unity and love. However, other families who attend the same church, hear the same sermons, pray around the same altar, and read out of the same Bible seem to be plagued with family stress. The delicate balance of relationships is upset by almost any problem that enters their little world.

158

The problems faced by Christian families are similar to those faced by all families in the culture. There is the problem of rebellion. This often comes in the lives of teenagers who are in the transition period between childhood and adulthood. There is the problem of divorce. Our culture has done everything it can to legalize, rationalize, and normalize divorce as an accepted way of life. However, the traumatic consequences of divorce on the family are still the same. There is the problem of alcohol and drugs. Since the surgeon general of the United States made his famous announcement on the harmful effects of smoking, 30 million Americans have kicked the habit. However, drugs and alcohol, which are worse than smoking, are still the popular vices of the day and make great appeals to young people trying to prove their adulthood and independence from parental domination.

The troubles that plague families may be discussed under five divisions: (1) problems with children, (2) problems with parents, (3) guideposts for healing, (4) principles of living in peace with each other, and (5) the principle of homeostasis.

What Every Child Deserves

Some years ago Dr. William Glasser wrote a book, *Reality Therapy*, in which he turned away from the permissive approach in dealing with the problems of children and laid out a much more assertive role for parents and therapists in which the key word is *responsibility*. More recently, Dr. James Dobson has written a book called *Dare to Discipline*. Both of these books are excellent, but Paul makes the point clearly and much more briefly in his references to children in the homes of the Christians in Ephesus.

Parental responsibility: Parents need to teach their children to obey: "Children, obey your parents in the Lord: for this is right." Moses did not think up the Ten Commandments on Mount Sinai, nor did God at that particular time decide to make up rules for civilization. These norms, or rules, have been a part of human nature since God made man in the Garden of Eden. One of these rules, which "is right," is that children must be taught to obey their parents in the Lord.

Parental honor: The second principle in raising children to be responsible adults is to teach them respect for their elders: "Honour thy father and mother; . . . that it may be well with thee."

There are five related areas of guidance that every child deserves to receive. (1) Every child needs to be taught *manners* and etiquette for the dinner table, the telephone, and the automobiles. (2) Every child needs to be taught *respect* for other people's property. (3) Every child needs to be taught *responsibility for his own behavior and circumstances.* The child who is allowed to grow up without ever picking up his own clothes, cleaning his room, or having responsibility in the home is not likely to have any strong feelings of responsibility in adulthood. (4) Every child needs to be taught *respect for his parents and family members.* A boy who does not honor his mother (or his sister) for who she is, is not likely to respect his girlfriend or wife. (5) Every child needs to be taught *respect for authority figures.*

A Warning Against Provoking

Paul suggests a warning and an admonition for fathers. A father's own behavior can provoke a child to disobedience or antisocial behavior: "And, ye fathers, provoke not your children to wrath." A father who causes his child to have an angry outburst should himself be punished instead of the child. Again, Paul admonishes fathers to be counselors and disciplinarians in the family: "Bring them up in the nurture and admonition of the Lord." Rearing children to be responsible adults and practitioners of the living faith in Christ is not a part-time vocation. The father needs to be an example in attitude and behavior. He also needs to spend uninterrupted periods of time with each individual child.

Guideposts for Healing

Fatigue, financial pressures, anxieties about aging, decisions that have backfired, and many more things contribute to the circumstances from which problems arise in families. However, the difference between a Christian home and a non-Christian home is not the absence or presence of problems, but the way these are faced. In a non-Christian home, destructive behavior, such as anger, violence, jealousy, and revenge, may be expected. But for the Christian home, Paul outlines a series of attitudes that become guideposts for healing when problems do arise.

Mercy: Most of us cannot make it in our homes by always receiving justice. Most of us need better than we deserve. We need the mercy of those in the family who are willing to love us in spite of our mistakes and give us the benefit of the doubt when we have done nothing to deserve it.

Kindness: Learning how to be kind to one another in a family is the essence of Christian happiness at home. Snarling, picking, yelling, and shouting only enlarge the problem, while kindness acts like the oil of the Holy Spirit in healing a wound.

Humility: Although a meek spirit is a Christian virtue, it does not come naturally and is one of the most difficult attitudes to learn sincerely and to demonstrate honestly, without the appearance of a performance.

Meekness: It is no sign of strength to be a loner. There is no lasting virtue in being completely independent of every other individual. God made man with the need for human relationship.

Long-suffering: Recent studies have indicated that among families who have suffered long sieges of terminal cancer the divorce rate is higher than it is in the general population. However, this problem need not be in the Christian home where the power of the Holy Spirit is present to supply strength for long-suffering.

Giving and forgiving: Perfectionists are difficult people to live with. They have no room for either giving or forgiving. It is unchristian to accept the forgiveness of Christ and then be unwilling to extend the same forbearance and forgiveness to those in our own family.

Preventing Quarrels

Although Paul's admonitions on the healing of quarrels in the family are helpful, a small amount of prevention is better than all of the healing balm in the world. In one paragraph, Paul suggests the principles to be followed for peace in the family.

Inner peace: "Let the peace of God rule in your hearts . . . and be ye thankful." When members of a family have inner peace, which comes from a right relationship with God, there is little need for serious family disruption. Momentary irritation, transient pressures, and an edge in the voice of the person who is frustrated and mentally fatigued, are a part of family living. One of the functions of the home is to serve as a place where, within limits, steam can be let off. However, this is altogether different from the crises that disrupt the stability of family relationships.

Happiness and joy: The first goal in family relations is to make the home a bulwark of love and emotional security. Paul suggests several ways this is done. (1) By learning how to use knowledge: "Let the word of Christ dwell in you richly in all wisdom." There is a vast difference between knowledge and wisdom. Knowledge knows how to behave while wisdom knows how to apply the knowledge in the situations of life. (2) In the Christian family there is singing: "teaching and admonishing one another in psalms and hymns and spiritual songs." It is easy to believe that a family who learns to sing together has developed a strong bond for living together. (3) The third suggestion is graciousness: "singing with grace in your hearts to the Lord." It is doubtful Paul had the quality of people's voices in mind when he admonished them to sing. He was calling for the melody of the heart (Eph. 5:19).

Christ is the Standard: "And whatsoever ye do in word or deed, do all in the name of the Lord Jesus" becomes the final test of any conversation and any relationship as to whether or not it invokes the smile and blessing of God.

Family Homeostasis

Homeostasis is the delicate balance of relationships in

the home. When the delicate balance of relationships is harmed, severe trouble may result.

In these verses, Paul makes suggestions to wives, husbands, and children on how to keep the beautiful balance there is in Christian family relationships. (1) Wives are to give deference to their husbands as the leader of the family: "Wives, submit yourselves unto your own husbands, as it is fit in the Lord." (2) Husbands must deserve their leadership in the family by the demonstration of their unconditional love for their wives: "Husbands, love your wives, and be not bitter against them." A husband is not the lord over his wife. He is her protector, colleague, and very best friend. (3) Children must learn obedience to their parents as the norm for family living: "Children, obey your parents in all things: for this is well pleasing unto the Lord." There are several results: The obedient child feels better about himself. The obedient child feels better about his parents. The obedient child feels better about life. The obedient child at home will soon be able to understand the meaning of obedience to the will of God: "For this is well pleasing unto the Lord."

Chapter 16

Divorce

Scriptural Stepping-stones

"A writing of divorcement"

> "It hath been said, Whosoever shall put away his wife, let him give her a writing of divorcement: but I say unto you, That *whosoever shall put away his wife, saving for the cause of fornication, causeth her to commit adultery:* and whosoever shall marry her that is divorced committeth adultery."

Matt. 5:31-32

*　　*　　*

"They that be whole need not a physician"

> "And it came to pass, as Jesus sat at meat in the house, behold, many publicans and sinners came and sat down with him and his disciples. And when the Pharisees saw it, they said unto his disciples, *Why eateth your Master with publicans and sinners?* But when Jesus heard that, he said unto them, *They that be whole need not a physician, but they that are sick.* But go ye and learn what that meaneth, I will have mercy and not sacrifice: for I am not come to call the righteous, but sinners to repentance."

Matt. 9:10-13

* * *

"Let her remain unmarried"

> "And unto the married I command, yet not I, but the
> Lord, *Let not the wife depart from her husband: but and if
> she depart, let her remain unmarried, or be reconciled to her
> husband:* and *let not the husband put away his wife.* But to
> *the rest speak I, not the Lord:* If any brother hath a wife
> that believeth not, and she be pleased to dwell with him,
> let him not put her away. And the woman which hath an
> husband that believeth not, and if he be pleased to dwell
> with her, let her not leave him. For the unbelieving hus-
> band is sanctified by the wife, and the unbelieving wife
> is sanctified by the husband: else were your children
> unclean; but now are they holy. But if the unbelieving
> depart, let him depart. A brother or a sister is not under
> bondage in such cases: but God hath called us to peace.
> For what knowest thou, O wife, whether thou shalt save
> thy husband? or how knowest thou, O man, whether
> thou shalt save thy wife?"

1 Cor. 7:10-16

The divorce rate in the Western world has been rising for
several decades. In 1957, the divorce rate per 1,000 population was 2.2. In 1967, the divorce rate per 1,000 population
was 2.7. In 1972, there was a 4.3 rate of divorce per 1,000
population, attributed by the Department of Health, Education, and Welfare people in Washington to the trend toward
no-fault divorce (U.S. Department of HEW, "Monthly Vital
Statistics Report").

This analysis does not account for the rapid rise in divorce in the most recent years and the fact that divorces in-

166

volving children are up dramatically. Also, there are more separations, desertions, and annulments than ever before. In many large cities, such as Los Angeles, more people seek to break marriages legally than seek to marry legally in most months of the year. In such widely diverse areas as Oklahoma City, Okla., and San Mateo County, California, marriage "deficits" are reported because of the increase in divorces, annulments, and separations. Yet neither of these places are "divorce havens" with easy laws to encourage out-of-state divorce.

In Western civilization there have been three phases in the history of the family. (1) The phase characterized by strong family unity and leadership. (2) Then came the time when family control over individual members was weakened, although the family unit remained strong. (3) Finally, family loyalty became replaced by individualism. In this kind of family organization there is *(a)* reduced importance on the marriage ceremony, *(b)* an increase in extramarital relationships, *(c)* acceptance of sexual permissiveness, *(d)* easy divorce, *(e)* childlessness, and *(f)* delinquency. (See Carl C. Zimmerman, "The Future of the Family in America," *Journal of Marriage and the Family,* July 1972.) Dr. Zimmerman believes that America, like Greece and Rome before it, is in the final stages of the shift into the era of the weak family with few personal loyalties and strong emphasis on individual rights and prerogatives.

This shift to individualism is not pronounced in Christian homes. But just because Christian families are a part of the greater general culture, all church homes are subject to the impact of changing norms in sexuality, marriage, and family.

This is why this study is of significance for all Christians in families!

The Bible and Divorce

The basic teaching on divorce in the Bible is in this Old Testament law: "When a man hath taken a wife, and married her, and it come to pass that she find no favour in his eyes, because he hath found some uncleanness in her: then let him write her a bill of divorcement, and give it in her hand, and send her out of his house" (Deut. 24:1).

The key phrase in this directive is "some uncleanness." In the days of Jesus there were two schools of thought on the meaning of "some uncleanness." (1) The conservatives believed "some uncleanness" meant adultery and nothing else. Even though a man like Ahab had a wife as mischievous as Jezebel, he was to stay with her and make the most of marriage unless she committed acts of adultery. (2) The liberal rabbis interpreted "some uncleanness" to mean anything from ineptness in the kitchen to rudeness in the parlor, friendliness on the street, or just a husband's desire to get rid of a wife who stood in his way of marrying a woman he found more to his liking.

Jesus clarified the meaning of "some uncleanness" once and for all for His followers. "It hath been said, Whosoever shall put away his wife, let him give her a writing of divorcement: but I say unto you, That whosoever shall put away his wife, saving for the cause of fornication, causeth her to commit adultery: and whosoever shall marry her that is divorced committeth adultery" (Matt. 5:31-32).

However, since the days of Jesus and especially in these modern times, there have been changing attitudes toward marriage. When Jesus began His statement on divorce with the phrase, "It hath been said . . . but I say unto you," it indicates that marriage has always been faced by the problem of compromise.

The changing views on marriage in the general culture have overtones in Christian homes. (1) Individual happiness has replaced stability as the major goal of marriage partners. There is no new friction in marriage these days, but there is an unwillingness among many couples to tolerate old frictions. (2) Another factor in changing attitudes on marriage is the acceptance of more frequent contact of marriage partners with friends and coworkers of the opposite sex. (3) The liberalization of divorce laws and changing public opinion about divorce have contributed to the fragility of the marriage bond. "No-fault" divorce laws in some states are a reversal of the usual pattern of easy-to-get-into and difficult-to-get-out-of marriages. (4) The functions of the family have undergone great changes. Sociologists like to point out that the family has lost, or greatly diminished, *(a)* its work function, *(b)* its educational function, *(c)* its protective function, *(d)* much of its recreational function, and even a great deal of *(e)* its child-care function. For many secular families the major ties are emotional; and emotions, to say the least, are not stable. There is nothing more important in a marriage than a determination that it shall persist.

Compassion, Judgment, and Forgiveness

We have literalized the command of Jesus on divorce in a way we have not applied to His other commandments. For instance, we do not pluck out an offending eye, cut off a guilty hand, give away our cloaks, never turn down a borrower, or always, under all circumstances, love our enemies. And we do judge others, directly contrary to the command of Jesus in Matt. 7:1, "Judge not, that ye be not judged." No doubt it is easier to administer law than love, to practice common sense in not giving away our cloak or our money, and to let humanitarian ideals restrain us from plucking out eyes and cutting off hands. But when it comes to the matter of divorce we tend to be harsh in our judgment.

On the other hand, in spite of all the efforts there are to rationalize, legitimatize, and normalize divorce as humane and unavoidable, we cannot ignore or circumvent the Christian principle of marriage as an indissoluble bond, a commitment for life. Yet today, in spite of what Jesus said about divorce, and what the church takes as a Christian principle of marriage, it is a fact that churches everywhere have divorced people within their memberships.

It cannot be an act of Christian love to condemn forgiven sinners to lives of spiritual and social misery because of the consequences of their decisions before they were converted. Along with Christian law there is also Christian love, and where there is judgment with love there is always room for forgiveness.

When Jesus came by and asked Matthew to leave his nefarious business and follow Him, it must have been a surprise to everyone but Jesus that he did. The occasion called for a celebration that turned out to be a dinner that in turn was attended by Matthew's sinner friends and criticized by all the orthodox religious people who believed more in being right than in doing good. From this story, there are several lessons that may be applied to forgiveness and love wherever it is practiced.

There is no one Christ cannot change through forgiveness: Matthew "arose, and followed him" (Matt. 9:9). The ramifications of *(a)* financial restitution, *(b)* government obligations, *(c)* the hostility of people, and *(d)* Matthew's materialistic life-style would seem to have made forgiveness difficult and a change of life almost impossible. Matthew, like many other people, seemed to be too far in to get out. But he did. "He arose, and followed him."

Forgiveness was followed by social acceptance: "Many publicans and sinners came and sat down with him and his disciples" at a dinner called to introduce Jesus to Matthew's friends. It is easier to forgive and depart than it is to forgive and get involved. It is a tribute to Jesus that Matthew felt comfortable in bringing his rough, worldly friends to dinner with Him. Jesus did not ask Matthew to turn against his friends as a price for forgiveness.

Not everyone was happy when Jesus fellowshipped with sinners: "When the Pharisees saw it, they said . . . Why eateth your Master with publicans and sinners?"

The point of view of the scribes and Pharisees is by no means extinct in our modern Christian Church. *(a)* They were more interested in judging than in forgiving. *(b)* They were more interested in their own righteousness than they were in helping sinners. *(c)* They were more interested in being right than doing good. *(d)* They were afraid of the possible consequences of accepting forgiven sinners into their fellowship.

Jesus set the norm for all churches: "I will have mercy, and not sacrifice: for I am not come to call the righteous, but sinners to repentance."

171

Religion, Marriage, and Remarriage

Studies on 25,000 couples have shown there were three times as many marriage failures among those with no religious affiliation as among those with a religious commitment. Even marriages between people of different religions have a lower failure level than those with no religion. One study compared divorced and happily married couples and found a higher percentage of the happily married couples had *(a)* a church wedding, *(b)* were church members, *(c)* and were active in Sunday School and church attendance *(d)* both before and during marriage.

The matter of remarriage: "Let not the wife depart from her husband: but and if she depart, let her remain unmarried, or be reconciled to her husband" (1 Cor. 7:10-11). To the husband or wife who is caught in the difficult experience of divorce or separation, Paul gives a command that he says came from the Lord. (1) Wives are not to leave their husbands, and husbands are not to "put away" their wives. (2) But if there is separation anyhow, there are two options. *(a)* "Let her remain unmarried," or *(b)* "be reconciled to her husband." This command is in harmony with the understanding of many Christian psychologists, pastors, and counselors, that two mature adults can make a marriage work if both of them want the marriage to work. Couples in stress do not need a book or a counselor if they can have total commitment to their marriage.

Believers married to unbelievers: "If any brother hath a wife that believeth not . . . let him not put her away. And the woman which hath a husband that believeth not . . . let her not leave him." It is interesting that Paul does not blame the Lord for his directive but takes the responsibility himself for what he is saying to divided homes: "Speak I, not the Lord."

Chapter 17

Marriage Has Its Limits

Scriptural Stepping-stones

"Treasure in earthen vessels"

> "But *we have this treasure in earthen vessels*, that the excellency of the power may be of God, and not of us."
>
> 2 Cor. 4:7

*   *   *

"Troubled . . . yet not distressed"

> "We are *troubled on every side, yet not distressed;* we are *perplexed, but not in despair; persecuted, but not forsaken; cast down, but not destroyed;* always bearing about in the body the dying of the Lord Jesus, that the life also of Jesus might be made manifest in our body. For we which live are alway delivered unto death for Jesus' sake, that the life also of Jesus might be made manifest in our mortal flesh. So then death worketh in us, but life in you. We having the same spirit of faith, according as it is written, I believed, and therefore have I spoken; we also believe, and therefore speak; knowing that he which raised up the Lord Jesus shall raise up us also by Jesus, and shall present us with you. For all things are for your sakes, that the abundant grace might through the thanksgiving of many redound to the glory of God."
>
> 2 Cor. 4:8-15

"Though our outward man perish"

> "For which cause we faint not; but though our outward man perish, yet *the inward man is renewed day by day.* For our light affliction, which is but for a moment, worketh for us a far more exceeding and eternal weight of glory; while we look not at the things which are seen, but at the things which are not seen: for the things which are seen are temporal; but the things which are not seen are eternal."
>
> 2 Cor. 4:16-18

Television and a much more accessible world have raised the marriage expectations of many young wives. Girls anticipating marriage may well fantasize their husband will have all the resoluteness, decisiveness, intelligence, sensitivity, and good looks of the national television or professional athletic heroes plus all the desirable and none of the undesirable characteristics of their father. When expectations are too high, disappointment is inevitable.

From the glamorized showcase of women in the mass media men may easily and understandably develop standards for their wives that cannot be met in real life. Many young men visualize their future wives as paragons of beauty, charm, poise, and elegance; sweet, kind, tender, and loving; plus all the unquestioned skills of a homemaker, ideal mother, and sweetheart. This view is unreal, but that is not the end of the problem. The add-ons also include responsibilities as gourmet cooks, small-appliance repair persons, drivers on call, buyers with professional management skills, bookkeepers, child psychologists, and counselors for their frustrated husbands. Also, the young wife is expected to be warm, tender, submissive, adjustable, agreeable, and subservient to the demands of her husband's career.

Against the backdrop of marriage expectations, one of the favorite verses of husbands and wives should be, "But we have this treasure in earthen vessels" (2 Cor. 4:7).

The Earthen Vessels of Marriage

Since marriage partners are human, it is important for husbands and wives to accept the limitations within each other and in their relationships with each other. Although this statement on "this treasure in earthen vessels" is given by Paul in the larger context of a discussion of the ministry, it has application directly to home and marriage.

First, it is important to remember that each marriage partner has personal limitations: (1) We are all human, which means we have serious lacks in physical qualities, intellectual understanding, emotional maturity, and spiritual strength. (2) We are limited by circumstances. (3) The possibility of emotional damage from childhood may bear serious consequences throughout marriage, particularly in the early years. (4) Changes beyond our control, such as death, terminal illness, or unusual and quick success by one of the marriage partners, may greatly restrict the marriage relationship. (5) Physical and emotional fatigue constitute the greatest single limiting factor in many marriages.

Second, there is confusion on role limits in many marriages: In many of today's child-centered homes, the child is treated like a family pet with the expectation that his major satisfactions will come from receiving things. As parents lavish more and more possessions on their children, their rooms take on the look of a toy store, and their minds take on the value system of a materialist who sees people as means for more personal satisfaction. This kind of child who grows into the marriageable years sees the marriage partner as one more source of meeting his or her needs.

Third, many marriages are limited by differing expectations: Specialized expectations always result in misunderstanding and can result in the total breakdown of the marriage. (1) Sometimes the marriage partner is asked to do things the husband or wife could do easily for themselves. (2) Sometimes the husband or wife expects their partner to do things they haven't even told them to do. (3) And sometimes responses are expected even when the marriage partner denies even wanting them. For instance, a wife may tell her husband to save money by not calling home on a trip and then become upset because he did not go ahead and call anyway.

Fourth, and finally, many marriages are limited by a faulty self-concept: The more understanding and agreement there is between marriage partners on expectations and on each partner's perception of himself, the more happiness there will be in the home. In fact, divorce is most often caused by differences in expectations and conflicts in self-concepts that have risen to an intolerable level. If the husband sees himself as witty, strong, and clever, and his wife sees him as dull, weak, and boring, trouble cannot be circumvented. But every marriage is limited. None is fully perfect.

The Paradoxes of Marriage

Give any family 25 years together, and there will be memorable high spots and unforgettable low spots. But many couples will report that tough times did something special for their marriage. That sounds like a contradiction, but it isn't.

There is the paradox of stress without distress: Hans Selye, the famous physician and teacher at the University of Montreal, has written an entire book to explain the paradox of stress and distress. A problem-free life would not be a life at all. Problems are a part of being alive. Where there is no stress there is death. Distress is stress that has become unpleasant and hurtful. Therefore, stress for one person may be distress for another.

There is the paradox of confusion without despair: "We are perplexed, but not in despair." Dr. Richard Meeth, in a message to Christian college presidents, outlined the downward steps in the successions of responses to the stress of living. The first of the four steps was confusion and the last was despair. Prayer, a good, healthy attitude, and positive action can clear up confusion. But despair is the last stop before complete collapse and death.

There is the paradox of misunderstanding without rejection: "Persecuted, but not forsaken." Any family has reached a mature level of relationships when the members can deal in a Christian-like manner with irregular, nonconformist behavior, and not reject the family member who is temporarily or permanently deviant.

There is the paradox of being knocked down but not knocked out: "Cast down, but not destroyed." Through the pilgrimage of family living there are falls, scuffs, and bruises. But from these experiences the family can rise to move on together. A famous football coach once stated, "The first basic lesson every football player learns is to get up just one more time."

Paul, who was hit hard many times, also knew he was never beaten and never ultimately defeated. He lost some battles, but it never crossed Paul's mind that he would lose the war.

The Philosophy of an Enduring Relationship

Every person has a philosophy, or a general point of view, on many subjects, including home and marriage. In this paragraph, Paul suggests the philosophy that kept him going in face of a life filled with difficult experiences. Here are some secrets of Paul's endurance.

Commitment to Christ, though a calculated risk, is worth the risk: There is risk in serving Jesus. Just as there is risk in serving Christ, there is a calculated risk in committing yourself to someone in marriage for better or for worse, "till death do us part." But a part of my philosophy on marriage is that it is worth the risk.

Paul never failed to remember the power of the Resurrection: Paul's philosophy made it possible to live courageously without fear. As Pope John Paul II flew off to Turkey at the height of the Iran crisis that involved the American hostages, he responded to the fears of his advisors for his safety by reminding them, "Our lives are in God's hands." There are times in the pilgrimage of life when husbands and wives need to join hands in mutual support of each other. In the face of a common obstacle we must remember that the power of the Resurrection is a source of adequate strength for life and is even more powerful than death.

Paul believed his life could generate thanksgiving in others and bring about glory to God: Through the years, our attitudes and patterns of behavior generate one of two responses from the people in our family—thanksgiving or hostility. *(a)* If we generate thanksgiving in our children, they will love us, respect us, and probably will adopt and internalize the values and priorities of our lives. *(b)* If we generate hostility in our children, they will either completely reject us or manipulate us for their own purposes. The way parents treat their children in the first 20 years of their lives will determine the way the children will treat them in the last 20 years of theirs.

Factors in Growth and Endurance

Every book has a final chapter, and every piece of music has a final eight bars. And so does marriage. To the needs of the closing time of life, Paul addresses three thoughts.

As the body fades, the soul grows: Although there is no way to prevent the body from fading, there are ways to keep the spirit growing. *(a)* There is the advantage of the long look. Older couples have seen it all before. They have ballast in their vessel. *(b)* There is the advantage of clear priorities. The older couple needs the companionship of each other, guaranteed basic subsistence, good health, and secure family ties. *(c)* There is the satisfaction of a fulfilled life. The children are grown. Life is filled with memories, little moments and big, that string together like an irregular strand of precious pearls.

Suffering in this world is not to be compared with the joy of the next: There comes a time when the fact of death must be faced. Either it will be faced in fear or in peace, but it must be faced. With complete peace of mind, Paul looked toward the

181

joy of the next world that would more than offset the penalties of living in an "earthen vessel" in this one. *(a)* There is the joy of our wealth at work for God after we are gone. A will left in favor of a Christian college is hard to beat as an eternal investment. *(b)* There is the joy of a family raised. *(c)* There is the joy of eternal life with Christ and the saints. *(d)* There is the joy of continued growth and development for eternity. Joy is not idleness. Joy comes not only from a state of mind, but also from having something to do, from continued maturation and fruitfulness. Whatever heaven is, it will not be a place of static idleness.

Paul's final secret of endurance was his ability to sort out the difference between the visible and the invisible: Assuming there is an adequate subsistence for daily needs, couples in the retirement years of their lives have less and less concern over material matters and more and more concern with the higher values of the unseen world. Love, loyalty, friendship, acceptance, and memories are some of the invisible things that become more important than cars, houses, clothes, and gourmet food.

Chapter *18*

The Congregation
as the Extended Family

Scriptural Stepping-stones

"The body . . . hath many members"

> "For as *the body is one, and hath many members,* and all
> the members of that one body, being many, are one
> body: so also is Christ."
>
> 1 Cor. 12:12

*   *   *

"Into one Spirit"

> "For by one Spirit are we all baptized into one body,
> whether we be Jews or Gentiles, whether we be bond or
> free; and *have been all made to drink into one Spirit.* For
> the body is not one member, but many."
>
> 1 Cor. 12:13-14

*   *   *

"Many members, yet but one body"

> "If the foot shall say, *Because I am not the hand,* I am not
> of the body; is it therefore not of the body? And if the ear
> shall say, *Because I am not the eye,* I am not of the body;
> is it therefore not of the body? If the whole body were an
> eye, where were the hearing? If the whole were hearing,

where were the smelling? But now hath God set the members every one of them in the body, as it hath pleased him. And if they were all one member, where were the body? *But now are they many members, yet but one body. And the eye cannot say unto the hand, I have no need of thee: nor again the head to the feet, I have no need of you.*"

1 Cor. 12:15-21

* * *

"Our comely parts have no need"

"Nay, much more *those members of the body, which seem to be more feeble, are necessary:* and those members of the body, *which we think to be less honourable, upon these we bestow more abundant honour;* and our uncomely parts have more abundant comeliness. For our *comely parts have no need:* but God hath tempered the body together, having given more abundant honour to that part which lacked: that there should be no schism in the body; but that the members should have the same care one for another. *And whether one member suffer, all the members suffer with it; or one member be honoured, all the members rejoice with it.*"

1 Cor. 12:22-26

The Spirit of Christ, our risen Lord, is in the earth, but the only body He has is the Church. And we believers are the Church. "And all the members of that one body, being many, are one body: so also is Christ" (v. 12).

As the body has an "I," or a unifying person, invisible but directly related to the body while separate from it, the Church

184

also has its great "I am," its central Life Force, its Fountainhead of spiritual vitality, who is Christ, the risen Lord.

As members of the Body of Christ we need to understand three things about the family support system: (1) Just as persons in the church need each other, families need each other. Just as there is no human being who can live for long in total isolation, no family can exist as a family by itself. (2) Just as persons in the church must respect each other, families in the Body of Christ must learn respect for each other's families. (3) Family understanding is an extended form of human understanding. Persons are understood best who are understood within the framework of their families.

Support from the Sacraments

At breakfast one morning a man who has reared a family of lovely children who have strong marriages and practice their faith, told me why he keeps going regularly to a church that is currently on hard times. He explained, "I know the sermons aren't very good, but it's our church, and it has a lot of things going for it besides preaching." A loving, caring church does have a lot going for it.

First, there is help from the sacrament of baptism: There are several implications in baptism as a support system of the church for the family. *(a)* Baptism means dying and rising again to a new life with Christ. This newness of life is described in Rom. 6:3-4. In the church, this newness of life is encouraged, fortified, and expanded. *(b)* Baptism also means incorporation into the Body of Christ. It is no more possible to be a lone Christian without the support of other Christians than it is to be a lone coal on the fire without the support of other coals. One guaranteed result of being a Christian is the support of the family of God. *(c)* Baptism also overcomes the barriers between races and nations. In the ancient world Jews and Gentiles at best tolerated each other and at worst lived in open hostility with each other. But in the family of Christ these barriers disappear. The support system of the church for the family breaks down the barriers with the weaponry of love and purity. *(d)* Baptism overcomes also the barriers between classes of people, the "bond or free."

And then there is blessing and help from the sacrament of the Lord's Supper: It could be that Paul is referring here to the words of Jesus when He said, "If any man thirst, let him come unto me, and drink. He that believeth . . . out of his belly shall flow rivers of living water. (But this spake he of the Spirit, which they that believe on him should receive . . .)" (John 7:37-39). But Paul may more likely have been referring to the sacrament of the Lord's Supper, which goes hand in hand with baptism as outward signs of inward grace. Baptism occurs once at the beginning of the new life in Christ, while the Lord's Supper is a continuing reminder of the Christian's source of grace in the death and resurrection of Jesus. Baptism represents forgiveness of sins, while the Lord's Supper is a means for the continual renewing of grace.

Support from Each Other

The human body needs each of its organs to function fully, whether they be small, large, visible, invisible, weak, strong, prominent, or unknown. The loss of any member makes it more difficult for all the others to function properly. Paul believed interdependency obtained in the Body of Christ also—"For the body is not one member, but many." This is the principle of unity in diversity. Love does not depend on everyone having the same views or even feeling alike toward each other. Love is a commitment that comes naturally to people who have unity of purpose.

Foot, Hand, Ear, and Eye

Someone has invented the word *homeostasis* to describe the delicate balance there is among all the organs and systems of the human body. Some are mystifyingly complicated and others less so; but they are all there, and each has its purpose. The secret of good health is not the individual functioning of each organ or system, but the delicate balance among all of them that produces a beautiful synchronization that results in the feelings of soundness.

Homeostasis in the Body of Christ would be upset if everybody wanted to be something he is not. Paul states, "If the foot shall say, Because I am not the hand . . . and if the ear shall say, Because I am not the eye, I am not of the body; is it therefore not of the body?" (vv. 15-16). The harmony of both the home and the support system in the church are seriously endangered if everybody wants to be something he is not. Everyone cannot be an eye, a hand, a foot, or an ear. Harmony in the home and the church are greatly enhanced when persons drop their pretenses and stop trying to be something other than what they are called or designed of the Lord to be. If spiritual homeostasis is upset by people trying to be someone they are not, it is even more upset by trying to homogenize everyone into a bland uniformity. The eye is very important and very beautiful. But if everyone were an eye, there would not be a body.

Furthermore, there is no member of the body who can make it on his own (v. 21). Meekness is knowing you need everyone else. And arrogance, which is the opposite of meekness, is rejecting the need for anybody else. Husbands need wives and wives need husbands; parents need children and children need parents.

The Weak and the Strong

Not every member of the Body of Christ is among the beautiful people. Some people are lovely while others are weak or uncomely. Concerning the support we receive from the weaker and stronger members, Paul made four observations.

There is need for the weaker members of the Body of Christ: If my neighbor is more powerful than I am, I may become suspicious and fearful of him. I may even become paranoid. If my neighbor is weaker than I am, I may be tempted to despise him and glory in my strength while I make fun of his infirmities. If we are equal, I could be tempted to outwit and manipulate him. What directives do I have for obeying or loving my neighbor, whether he is weaker, stronger, or equal to myself? Only one! I obey and I love because we are both members of the Body of Christ.

There are the beautiful people in the Body of Christ: There are some people who need no advantage of staging, packaging, or image building. They are strong, attractive, decisive. Other people tend to turn toward them for leadership. Thus, in the weak and the strong, there is mutual support from members of the Body of Christ.

There is support from the Body of Christ because of mutual commitment: In Paul's view there are three results in the mutuality to be found within the Body of Christ. *(a)* "Members should have the same care one for another" (v. 25). What is more supportive than to be accepted into a body of people who really care for each other! *(b)* "Whether one member suffer, all the members suffer" (v. 26). And that's the way it is in the Body of Christ, when one member is in distress all the other members are affected. *(c)* If "one member be honoured, all the members rejoice" (v. 26). Sometimes it takes more grace to enjoy the successes of friends than it does to suffer with them in their defeats and tragedies. But in the Body of Christ, the members rejoice with each other even when the success belongs to someone else.